The Healing of Humanity

ALSO BY PAULINE EDWARD

Spirituality/*A Course in Miracles*

The Movement of Being

Choosing the Miracle

Leaving the Desert: Embracing the Simplicity of A Course in Miracles

Making Peace with God: The Journey of a Course in Miracles *Student*

Astrology and Numerology

Astrological Crosses: Exploring the Cardinal, Fixed and Mutable Modes

The Power of Time: Understanding the Cycles of Your Life's Path

L'Hermès: Dictionnaire des correspondances symboliques, with Marc Bériault and Axel Harvey

The Healing of Humanity

Pauline Edward

Desert Lily Publications
Montreal, Canada

© 2017 Pauline Edward

Published by Desert Lily Publications, Montreal, Canada

All rights reserved. No part of this work may be reproduced or used in any form or by any means, electronic, digital or mechanical, including photocopying, recording or any retrieval system, without the prior written permission of the publisher.

Cover design: Pauline Edward
Editorial consultation: Veronica Schami

Library and Archives Canada Cataloguing in Publication

Edward, Pauline, 1954-, author
    The healing of humanity / Pauline Edward.

Includes bibliographical references.
Issued in print and electronic formats.
ISBN 978-1-927694-04-6 (softcover).--ISBN 978-1-927694-05-3 (Kindle).--ISBN 978-1-927694-06-0 (EPUB)

    1. Edward, Pauline, 1954-. 2. Course in miracles. 3. Spiritual life. I. Title.

BP605.C68E37 2017   299'.93   C2017-901894-9
                                                                                                               C2017-901895-7

Contents

Preface vii
Introduction 1
1. Once Upon a Time 9
2. The Story of Man 25
3. Waking Up to Reality 37
4. The Game Changer 53
5. A Helping Hand 69
6. Two by Two 81
7. Calls for Love 99
8. The Purpose of the Body 117
9. More Than a Body 129
10. Breaking the Isolation 139
11. A New Frontier for Humanity 149
An Invitation 166
Flowers in the Desert 167
Bibliography 169
Ego Flare-up Emergency Extinguishers 170
Tips for Working with Guidance 172
About the Author 183

Preface

To Write, or not to Write

While I was working on the final chapters of my last book, *The Movement of Being,* I received a clear message indicating that it was time to wrap it up and move it along to publication. At the time, I felt relieved of the task. As much as I enjoy writing and the profound sense of satisfaction that comes with the completion of a book, writing a book is, after all, a lot of work. I also thought this to mean that I was finished with writing, which is a perfect example of the trouble one can get into when indulging in independent thinking. For a moment—one of millions of such moments—I forgot that for real change to be experienced, independent thinking will need to be abandoned.

Since it is not only highly valued but also deeply ingrained in our human experience, thinking is an activity that is nearly impossible to avoid. For the most part, thinking is automatic, and as such, more often than we would like to admit, lacking in the essential intelligence that conscious awareness, a state that is experienced in the absence of thinking, would otherwise provide. Unless we consciously pay attention to the activities in which our mind is engaged, we have little control over the stuff churned out by our prolific mental machines, and mine, I dare say, is a well-oiled machine. Thinking is essentially a habit and a bad one at that.

We think. We think about everything we do, everything we did and everything we are about to do. We act on our thinking, and then we think some more. Until we pay attention and catch ourselves in the act, thinking is nearly impossible to curb. However, those familiar with *A Course in Miracles,* the Raj materials or similar teachings know that thinking can be a problem because it interferes with listening. In other words, thinking blocks reception. Without listening, there can be no shift in perception, no expanded awareness, thus no real change. In the absence of quiet listening, the experience of awakening remains unavailable.

Still, despite knowing better, I had effectively thought myself out of writing, an activity that had been very helpful for my learning and understanding, and, in a way, had become an integral part of who I am. When I eventually did take the time to turn to guidance, it was suggested that a break from writing might be a good idea; I had earned it. At the same time, it was pointed out that my writing days were not yet over, and there would be more books to come—that's "books" with an "s." *Yikes!*

As you may know from personal experience, guidance—the still, small voice within—does not coerce, demand, manipulate, frighten or insist. Out of respect for our innate, though perhaps slumbering, sanity and our freedom to choose, it merely invites us to look at things in a different way. Most of all, its voice is quiet, a gentle whisper, never loud or overpowering; it can easily be drowned out by the "other" voice, the one that would rather do things independently, the one that wants to take credit for its accomplishments. In a moment of receptive listening, I had to agree that taking a break from writing was probably a good idea. As for the part about the books with an "s," now that was an entirely different matter. *We'll see*, I replied, and then I chose to leave that tidbit aside for the time being. Considering that my writing ambitions had originally been aimed at the publication of one novel, one book at a time was about as much literary output as I could handle. I may have produced several books, but I am an exceedingly slow writer. When work on this book began, the writer in me slowed to a crawl then quickly stumbled and stalled.

After the manuscript of *The Movement of Being* had been placed in the hands of the editor, I began to feel lost. Without a work in progress, I didn't know what to do with myself. The previous year, in the hope of addressing a health issue, I had begun to experiment with a plant-based diet, and so in my newfound spare time, I eagerly researched and tested new recipes. It was fun to discover the many plant-based alternatives that had been developed by creative and adventurous chefs since my vegan days in the seventies. Still, feeling as though I didn't know what to do about anything anymore, I asked for help from my guide (referred to as "my Friend" throughout this book).

Always ready to shed light, my Friend pointed out that I was having difficulty adjusting to the new perspective on life and the world that I had been discovering through my studies. While I was beginning to open up and see in a different way, I was also attempting to understand the experience by grabbing onto anything I could relate to from memory. I was looking for something with which I was familiar to fill that void, or that sense of not knowing where I was, where I was going or, more importantly, who I was or who I was becoming. Cooking was a fun, creative activity I had always enjoyed, something with which I was familiar. Being quite lost, I did a lot of cooking!

Besides my culinary experiments, while on my writing sabbatical I searched for a good book to read, hopefully in the genre that had so inspired me years ago, like Thomas Merton's *Seven Storey Mountain*, yet something in harmony with my updated perspective on the meaning of life. After searching through new and old titles without finding anything that resonated with my changing views, I decided—all on my own, of course, without first running it by my wise Friend—that perhaps I should, once again, attempt a work of fiction. I would write that book I wanted to read. When I did get around to checking in with guidance—I may be slow, but I am capable of learning—I got the thumbs up for the novel. To refresh and update my fiction writing skills, I immersed myself in the study of the craft. Soon, I was hard at work on my new novel: Green Tea and Miracles. I was pleased. I designed a working cover, developed a basic story line and setting, created histories and traits for a group of characters and then proceeded to write the first couple of chapters. Back to writing, I was quite happily distracted.

Meanwhile, e-mails from readers began to trickle in. Most were enquiring as to whether there would be a next book and, if so, when it might be available. Deeply touched by the kind feedback and encouraged to continue writing, I responded to their enquiries by stating that there were no plans for another book in the genre but that I was instead hard at work on a novel. A work of fiction would allow for more flexibility in expressing the message that needed to be conveyed, or so I *thought*.

After several weeks of writing and rewriting the first couple of chapters, it occurred to me that I had become stuck; I was trapped in a set-up loop with no story in sight. So I did what I usually do when I become undecided or stuck: I stopped what I was doing and set the writing project aside. *Father*, I asked—finally!—*please let me know what you would like me to do*. And then I was quiet. Between working with clients and everyday tasks, I spent as many quiet moments as I could in silent listening, usually during my daily walks, which had become a form of walking meditation. Patiently, I waited for clarification.

As the weeks passed, I realized that, while I was quite willing to continue with the work of fiction, I was just as willing never to write another word again. I was content to sit on the balcony and let myself be infused by the infinite beauty of the newly planted flower pots filled with peach begonias, red geraniums, purple salvia and pink verbena. It was early summer; the grey of a very long, cold winter was being painted over by the multi-coloured beauty of nature's renewed awakening. The ducks and the geese had returned to nest on the island nearby. With open windows, I could hear the lively early morning wake-up call of the robins. Throughout the day, the lively *cheer, cheer, cheer* of the cardinals reminded me that there is a place in creation for all, even those that stand out like sore thumbs. I didn't need to write; I was at peace, and there was nowhere else I wanted to be.

When I wasn't in meditation or in contemplative awe of the movement of creation, the normal business of life continued. One day, clearly in answer to my prayer, while reading an article on fiction writing, it suddenly occurred to me why I had become stuck. My story would not work the way I had set it up; the story would need to be restructured. Soon after, I awoke one morning with the clear idea that I needed to pick up where *The Movement of Being* had left off. The work of fiction would be placed on the back burner. I had initially *thought* incorrectly; evidently, I was not entirely finished with writing. True, it had been a much-needed break, but it was now time to return to the keyboard.

The Attraction of Distraction

Given that I enjoy writing, it might follow that I dove right into this new book project without hesitation, with great energy and enthusiasm. Well, not quite. Since writing has become a way of connecting with inner guidance and one of the ways in which I can be in the quiet centre within, any hidden resistance to being in that precious space was bound to surface. And since I had been experiencing increasing appreciation for being in that quiet place, resistance surfaced with uninhibited vigour!

Why did I encounter resistance? Writing is an activity that provides clarity and understanding; at least this has been my experience. As my understanding was growing, it was becoming increasingly difficult to ignore the new learning that was emerging, a radical new learning that was requiring that I abandon all of my long-held beliefs and self-definitions. The message was growing so clear that it was becoming nearly impossible to ignore. Who wants to stare at the truth when fantasy still holds a certain appeal? Who is willing to abandon the familiar in exchange for a great unknown, especially when there are no guarantees that another way exists? Why give up what I think I know to be true when what I think I know seems to work relatively well?

So, it was not surprising that resistance was expressed in the form of mundane, worldly distractions. This was not surprising because 2015 was for me a number 3 Personal Year, and in numerology, the 3 is the number of creativity, joy, sociability and communications, but also chaos and distractions. I like to refer to the 3 as the ego's favourite number. It might be accurate to say that the ego's favourite sport is distraction, while its favourite climate is chaos. Being more comfortable with the structure, orderliness and productivity of the 4, I must admit that I am not overly fond of the chaotic nature of the 3. However, despite my preference for all things orderly, I stumbled headfirst into a stretch of enjoyable distractions, albeit tailored to my number 4 temperament, that is, relating to all things house and home, work and organization.

The first big distraction came in the form of a wild goose chase for a solution to the rock-hard ceramic flooring in my tiny condo kitchen. After several visits to the flooring store, hours spent at the computer playing with various samples and several brainstorming sessions with the sales rep, I found my solution at Costco. It seemed as though someone above was looking out for me, for there they were, in the first aisle, piles of cushioned floor mats, perfect for my needs, and saving a whole lot of money in the process.

You might think that was the end of my distractions, and I was now free to get back to the quiet place within and enjoy writing a book destined to shake the ego from its comfortable position as the predominant voice in my head. Not quite! Having underestimated the length of my floor, I returned the mat I had purchased and exchanged it for the longer model. Next, I returned that mat and exchanged it for another colour. Then I thought—notice the distracting activity of thinking—a long one and a short one would work, so back to the store I went. Then back to the store for a pair of long ones. You get the idea. I will spare you the details of what happened when I discovered rust in the bottom of my kettle, and then when I decided to replace my Teflon wok with a healthier ceramic alternative. After several months spent shopping online, ordering items, deciding they weren't adequate and returning them to their respective stores, I finally settled down. It's a wonder that the credit card company had no trouble keeping track of my purchases and returns. Did I mention that I detest shopping?

What does any of this have to do with awakening? Nothing and everything. While I was tempted to delete this section from the book, in the end, my Friend pointed out that it served the purpose of illustrating how even fun distractions are just that, distractions. As we will see, turning to the quiet centre within and listening for truth can be unsettling, while being sucked into mundane distractions is easy, even automatic. Eventually, without too much effort, in a calm and orderly fashion, I was able to rein in the senseless distractions of my wandering mind.

With a fresh cup of tea on the desk, made with water boiled in a rust-free kettle, from a kitchen fitted with a pair of long, cushy mats, after a hearty breakfast of tofu scrambled in a brand new ceramic pan, I forgave myself for my temporary folly and happily returned to writing. Oh, but wait a minute. If you thought this distraction-filled period ended with a quick press of the Enter key, a moment of silence and a fresh cup of tea, you would be wrong! I was only halfway through that number 3 year; there were more distractions to come!

First, I found myself accepting an invitation to join our condo association—something entirely outside my field of expertise. But hey, any distraction is a good distraction, right? I was given the task of heading up the gardening committee, an activity that was much more up my alley. With autumn came the task of dehydrating my veggies for the winter months. Any spare time that remained was spent on posting recipes for my food blog, which I suppose could be considered a form of writing. Next, I gave my website a major overhaul, a side trip that was actually justifiable since it needed to be converted to a responsive site.

Toward the end of that year of pleasant distractions, I started to feel the need to settle down and focus on work. With a number 4 year around the corner, I looked forward to a life of ordered simplicity, the 4 being the number of work, structure, health and family. On the first day of the new year, I wrapped up my year-end accounting and pulled out my notes. It felt good to finally get back to writing. However, I had barely revised the first couple of chapters when, once again, I hit more resistance, this time, ironically, in the form of an infection that was resistant to antibiotics. If simple distractions weren't going to keep me from writing, then a visit to death's door certainly would. We'll save that story for a later chapter.

It wasn't until the end of January that I returned my attention to the book. Resistance notwithstanding, this book was going to get written, no matter how long it took. Once again, I forgave myself.

On our journey of awakening, we are never condemned for our dalliances, and it is never too late to turn our attention within. Thank God! What matters is that once we realize that we have lost our direction, we make the necessary adjustment, and the adjustment is simple to make, for it is impossible to be truly lost.

I would like to express my deepest thanks to Raj for answering our call for help. Words cannot express the depth of my gratitude for your love and especially your patience in helping us with our awakening. Thank you, Paul Tuttle, and members of the Northwest Foundation for *A Course in Miracles* for making this help available to everyone around the world at a time when it is most needed and appreciated.

Not only are we sent teachers when we are ready to learn, we are also sent friends with whom to share the journey. I thank the Father for having placed a few dear souls in my neighbourhood so that together we can support each other on our journey Home. Thank you, Michael Miller and Robin Michel, for proofing the manuscript and Veronica Schami for your editorial wisdom. A big hug of gratitude to Helena Basso for nudging me along when I thought I could not get through this book.

Thank you to my clients for asking those questions that push me to find answers to what seem like unanswerable questions, and thank you for sharing the beauty of the unfolding of your Being.

Thank you, thank you, thank you.

Introduction

*"Perhaps there IS another way to look at this.
What can I LOSE by asking?"* (ACIM, Chap. 30, p. 685)

A Course in Miracles

Although this is the fifth book in which I share my journey with the teachings of *A Course in Miracles* (ACIM, the Course), it is not necessary to have read the previous four books, nor even to be familiar with the Course to appreciate its message. There are as many paths Home as there are paths away from Home, so in the matter of awakening, there is no one-size-fits-all formula. By the same token, if the Course—or any other spiritual teaching—appeals to you, it does not make you any more likely to experience awakening than one for whom that teaching holds no appeal. Whether it includes a spiritual component or not, any path that leads to the full awareness of the nature of being is a suitable path. Ultimately, it is the experience of the Love that is the Source of our being that matters.

If this book has called to you and you wish to skip over the first four in the series, by all means, jump right in. Nowhere does it say that everyone must get on the train at the same station; you get on the train at the stop nearest you. Only the destination—awakening—is the same for everyone. Because my journey has been long and tortuous, at least as viewed from my current perspective, it does not mean that others should follow the same path; in fact, to do so might add unnecessary length to a journey that need not be more than a moment in time. For, how long does it take to turn within to where the truth simply awaits our attention? How long does it take to choose peace and say yes to love?

There is a shift taking place in the world today; I see it in my consultation work with clients. Humanity is at a turning point; many souls are seeking release from far too long a time spent in obscurity and ignorance. Answers are being sought in all manner of teachings, from science to spirituality. What is needed is a simple, clear path to the truth, and what is being discovered is that this path lies within each individual who walks the earth today. It is a journey without distance, as the Course teaches, and the destination—an experience of full conscious awareness—is available to everyone, without exception. The truth is simple; it is accessible to every person, in any situation, regardless of circumstance, whether mundane or spiritual, for true vision can have no boundaries.

For many who are seeking an experience of awakening, or for those who are wondering if there might be a better way of being in the world, there eventually emerges a curiosity to know the true meaning of this journey we refer to as our life. What is the purpose of existence? Is there more to be experienced? How can that which is essentially spirit be experienced in a material world? How can we see what is divine in a brother when he behaves in a way that is clearly anything but divine? What is the meaning of awakening? How is the healing of humanity even possible in this time of confusion and chaos?

Although in my experience *A Course in Miracles* has provided answers to these questions, it has also changed me, and it has done so in ways that I am still discovering. It has changed me so profoundly that I sometimes wonder who I am, yet I have no inclination to go back to who I once was. However, I also realize that the Course is not an easy book to read, and it may not be the path for everyone. Most of my clients familiar with the Course have admitted to finding it almost, if not completely, impossible to read. Many never make it beyond the first couple of pages; most will probably never pick it up again. Sometimes there is shame associated with this admission, a sense of failure for not having been able to understand this increasingly popular new spiritual work.

These are sentiments with which I am familiar, having wondered if I had suddenly become dyslexic when I first read the big blue book. As expressed in my previous works, the Course was extremely difficult for me to read, let alone understand. It was only by sheer force of will that I made it through a first reading, after which I realized that I had hardly grasped any of its meaning. To this day, I do not grasp all of its psychological or biblical references; thankfully, that is not its purpose, nor is such understanding necessary. Having accepted that my brain functions in a linear fashion, I no longer berate myself for lacking the ability to appreciate complex, multi-layered metaphors. I have learned to love myself just the way I am, with my current levels of both understanding and ignorance. This is the best place to be because it is where true learning can be experienced, and the best learning is always fostered in a climate of love.

Over time—probably more time than I care to admit—the core message of the Course began to seep through the dense resistance of my unsophisticated intellect, and slowly, very slowly, a deep inner knowing began to emerge. I learned that it is not the container but rather the content that matters; it isn't the book but the meaning of the message it conveys to the reader that matters. What is important is how a teaching affects the student, how it heals the mind and how it shapes the way we are in the world. What truly matters is how we are with each other, for this is where the healing of humanity begins.

For those who have felt intimidated by a first attempt at reading the Course, you may find the "Sparkly" edition more accessible. (References in this work are from that edition of the Course.) Having undergone fewer edits, especially in the early chapters, it reflects more closely the original conversational tone between its author, Jesus, also known as Raj, and its scribe, Helen Schucman. Fortunately, it is not necessary to understand every line in the book. It may be helpful to see *A Course in Miracles* not so much as a book to be studied, learned, discussed, memorized and regurgitated but more as a nudge or a trigger. The Course invites us to consider that maybe, just maybe, there is another way of seeing, and ultimately, of *being* in the world.

A Course in Miracles is a big book and, yes, it is written in a style that might appeal to those of a somewhat more sophisticated, academic or analytical mind. But it is not entirely written in a complex style. In fact, its essential message is clearly expressed in very simple terms, and when read from the heart, it becomes clear that its Source is love. Having learned to appreciate myself despite my intellectual and poetic limitations, I have come to understand that love is the essence of all life, which includes my life and your life, and anything less than a direct experience of this love represents a condition that requires correction, or a *miracle*, as the Course defines it.

This book is meant as much for individuals who are not engaged in an active spiritual quest as it is for students of *A Course in Miracles* and other teachings. Effort has been made to use simple language, at least as simple as is possible, given the nature of the subject at hand. It may answer some of the questions asked by an increasing number of people today, or perhaps it will rouse questions that will lead to the discovery of answers. Where there is a question, an answer is always close by. It may also be helpful for the spiritual seeker wanting to learn how to interact more easily and more appropriately with those who are not engaged in a similar pursuit. In other words, it explores how to be *in* the world without being *of* the world.

In Answer to a Call for Help

No amount of studying, analysis of theory or discussion of theology, spirituality or metaphysics will deliver results unless the student is ready for its message. In other words, we cannot appreciate or accept new meaning without the desire, and especially the readiness, to consider it. This means that we do not actually seek to learn anything new, but rather to clarify and validate our current level of emerging knowing, and this clarification can come in any number of ways. One thing is certain, when the student is ready, the right teacher will come along, be it a book, a poplar tree bending and yielding to the wind, a sign on the side of a bus or the strains of a beautiful piece of music. This must be so, for love will always respond to a call for help in the most helpful and appropriate manner.

In my case, there came a point when the approaches I had been using to study the Course no longer provided clarification. In fact, my studies, though sincere and wholly dedicated, had begun to pose more problems and questions than answers. I felt lost, confused and alone; mostly, I had grown tired of studying. I had reached a threshold of unknowing in my learning, and it seemed that answers were nowhere to be found. It was at that moment that I was introduced to the "Raj Material." If it had been brought to my attention any sooner, I have no doubt that I would have rejected it outright. This new material came at exactly the right moment, when I needed it most, when, out of a desperate need for answers, resistance was at its weakest, and so it came when I was most ready to receive and appreciate it.

I point this out simply for the reader who is curious to know which path I have followed. Of the countless teachings explored throughout the decades-long journey of my life, it is the Raj Material that has been the most remarkable in that it has been the most effective in leading to clear, intimate experiences of truth. It is the teaching that resonated with my desire and readiness for a radically new way of seeing but also of *being*. It provided the clarification I needed in my study of *A Course in Miracles*, which then enabled me to have experiences like no other in my life. Because this is the path that has worked—and continues to work—for me, it does not necessarily mean that this is the appropriate path for everyone. In time, each person finds the teaching or the path that works for him or her.

On a journey of awakening, a teaching does not really teach anything new; it simply helps reveal a readiness to go beyond our current level of knowing. Since the truth is an integral part of our being, and our Source is eternal, it does not need to be taught; it simply lies in waiting for that moment when we are ready to welcome and eventually embrace it. A true teaching or teacher will serve to lead us to the truth that lies within. Being awake is natural and being asleep, or anything less than fully awake, is not; what is natural will inevitably emerge and what is not will simply fade away. While an intellectual understanding of a teaching may be helpful in grabbing our attention and stimulating our curiosity about the truth, ultimately it is the experience that is important. *A Course in Miracles* invites us to seek this experience.

> A universal theology is impossible, but a universal experience is not only possible but necessary… The ego will demand many answers that this course does not give. It does not recognize as questions the mere form of a question to which an answer is impossible. The ego may ask, "How did the impossible occur?", "To what did the impossible happen?", and may ask this in many forms. Yet there is no answer; only an experience. Seek only this, and do not let theology delay you. (ACIM, Preface, p. v)

A Word about Words

Language is one of the wonderful tools we have at our disposal that allow us to share experiences and connect with each other; however, it is not without its limitations. Unless one is a gifted poet, when attempting to put into words certain experiences, especially the deeply mystical, sometimes language simply fails. At times, failure to convey meaning effectively has the unfortunate effect of causing misunderstandings, alienation or even open conflict. Perhaps if I were a gifted poet, the task would be much easier, but since this is not the case, I am bound by the limitations of my current writing skills.

For language to be an aid rather than an obstacle to sharing, I have found it best not to focus too much on the words themselves, but simply to try to grasp a sense of their meanings—in other words, to read from the heart rather than through the filters of the intellect. One of the benefits of this shift in perspective is that less resistance and doubt are encountered, allowing for ease of communication or, perhaps more accurately, allowing for true communion. While the heart simply *knows* the truth, the intellect is inclined to require, or even demand, proof, perhaps as an indication of its inability to experience true knowing. I have found that being from the heart can be a helpful and fruitful approach with most things in life, not only with reading and with studying but especially when engaging with others. The truth is that the heart is the only place from which we can experience all that is being in the moment because love knows no boundaries.

Given the unique application of language as used in parts of this book, it might be helpful to clarify certain word choices. As such, it will be easier to appreciate the true meaning of what is being shared without becoming stuck on the use of words. Although this work uses language that is primarily Christian and Western in style, this does not mean that terms with equivalent meanings cannot be found in other teachings and cultures. For the sake of simplicity and expediency, and also not being a scholar of theology, I have chosen to use words with which I am familiar. Also, because Christian and Western terms have been used, it does not necessarily follow that these words hold the traditional meanings associated with them. Most of these terms—God, miracle, Kingdom of Heaven, awakening, Christ, Reality, being, ego, Holy Spirit, guidance—are introduced in the early chapters and presented in a context that hopefully will remove any ambiguity about their meaning in the present work.

So it is that this book more or less picks up where the last one left off—perhaps with a small gap in time during which my desire to experience the truth was strengthened and clarified. It contains a sprinkling of personal anecdotes, most of which are quite ordinary, even trivial; there is no major drama in my life, only the desire to continue on a quiet journey of awakening. This certainly does not make for a captivating read; there are no major challenges to be overcome, no extraordinary accomplishments—not much for which the ego can take credit, not much from which other egos can borrow. In other words, a boring read from an ego perspective. Nonetheless, they are the events of my life, and it is by choosing another way of seeing—or the miracle—in all situations, including the most commonplace, that awakening can occur. The truth is available in all circumstances, and so it is toward our day-to-day life that our attention needs to be turned, for that is where the key to awakening resides.

For the sake of those who are not familiar with *A Course in Miracles* and for those who have not read my previous books, some topics have been revisited, such as how to join with your guide. For the sake of illustration, some stories have also been repeated. Feel free to skip over those parts with which you are familiar. However, sometimes it can be helpful to review what we think we know, and in the process, trigger new insights. As boundaries of awareness are weakened, vision expands, and understanding is refreshed.

This book might have been subtitled *How Not to Think Your Way into the Kingdom of Heaven* or *How to Be in the Presence of God in the Middle of Traffic* or *Why Begonias Seem to Express more Intelligence than Humans* or *Why Peace Isn't as Boring as It Sounds*. I leave it up to you, dear reader, to choose, or even make up, your own subtitle.

CHAPTER 1

Once Upon a Time

The Power of Myth

Storytelling has long been an integral part of how we learn about history, culture, morals and life in general. As writers, we are taught that to capture and sustain the reader's attention, a good story must contain conflict. I am told that the same is true of a good piece of music. Think of any story you have read or any movie you have watched and enjoyed, and you will recognize that the main character—the hero of the story—has had to overcome seemingly insurmountable challenges. Our most popular stories are popular because they stimulate a range of emotions, such as elation, excitement, anticipation, terror and fear. The successful overcoming of obstacles, even if it comes at the cost of the lives of others, is usually portrayed as requiring above-average courage, self-sacrifice, perseverance, determination and great effort on the part of the hero. As we become desensitized by repeated exposure to violence, tragedy and drama, each new story must present a more vigorous form of the battle. No one seems to have a problem when the villain brutally meets his end; in fact, the successful defeat of evil is often accompanied by jubilation and a sense of satisfaction, no matter the devastation, destruction or violence.

While researching the craft of contemporary storytelling, I was surprised to find that the old formula of fiction writing had not changed much. Threats to the status quo, conflict and drama are still the primary ingredients of a good story. As much as humanity has learned and grown, the battle of good versus evil remains at the heart of every good story, except that now it is dressed up with more daring heroic acts. This is particularly evident in the film and television industry where storylines have been almost completely overshadowed by special effects. The greater the emotional charge, the better the story. I skimmed through novels, watched movies and television series, fast-forwarding through the violence and never-ending chase scenes but found very little that was inspiring in the world of storytelling. I could not find a story that satisfied my unrelenting curiosity about another way of being for humanity.

The success of a new television show can pretty much be gauged by how much it appeals to me; if I like it, it will most likely be canned; if I dislike it, it will probably be successful, which is what happened with one series that caught my attention. *Touch*, created by Tim Kring, centres on a young autistic boy who uses numbers to communicate with his father. All of his communications serve one purpose: to help resolve issues between individuals. The goal of each story is to connect people so that broken relationships can be healed and harmony can be restored. It is essentially a message of love, although oddly—or perhaps not, depending on the lens through which one looks—it is classified as a thriller. At first, I enjoyed where the writers were going with the series, finding it rather boldly enlightened, so much so that I saw how it might change how people experience their relationships. I even imagined how it could contribute to the healing of humanity. Judging from online reviews, I wasn't the only one to feel this way about the show. Perhaps this sounds naive, but where healing is concerned, we might want to remain open to whatever works.

Apparently, healing, harmony and the absence of conflict pose a threat to the status quo. As I watched the series, I couldn't help but suspect the inevitable; in all likelihood, what was a hopeful storyline would be defiled with the injection of a self-serving, corrupt government or corporate conspiracy subplot. There was just too much good in these stories to hold interest for very long. Evil, danger, conflict, war, violence, anger, greed, hate and vengeance sell. We love our dramas. Peace, harmony and love are not thrilling, so they are not good sellers. Still, I was excited when the second season began, but my excitement was short-lived. Unfortunately, I couldn't get past the first episode. The plot shifted in exactly the direction I had suspected: the battle between good and evil, including as much violence as can be crammed into forty minutes of television. What a shame, I thought, and again, as shown by comments made by other viewers on the Internet, I was not alone in my disappointment. I had truly seen potential in the series, for it was, after all, about what humanity needs the most at this critical time: the healing power of love.

We can't really blame the writers for the direction of these storylines since they are bound by the requirements established by those who sign their paycheques, the network managers, who are bound by an obligation to their shareholders. Although it is tempting to blame the networks for their production decisions, in the end it is the viewer—the consumer—who holds all the power. If no one watches a show, advertisers will not invest, the network will not make any money, writers and actors will not be paid and the inevitable outcome is that the show will be cancelled. If television shows and movies are filled with violence and other unenlightened behaviour, it is because a sufficient number of viewers have chosen to watch them. More viewers and better ratings mean higher revenues, and so the show lives on to see another season. Face it, who would be interested in a story without its fair share of drama and conflict? Even dressed up in the latest high-tech special effects, it would likely fail at the box office. What is disturbing about this conclusion is that it says more about the state of humanity than the entertainment industry, which is, ultimately, at the mercy of the consumer.

The Most Important Story

It doesn't take much research to realize that, just as in our favourite myths and stories, drama is the stuff of our everyday lives. In fact, it is what we are accustomed to—and what we actively seek out—whether we are conscious of it or not. The drama of our lives embodies the ubiquitous battle of good versus evil, a battle we gladly accept and engage in for the sense of accomplishment and satisfaction it provides. We compete for a greater share of the pie. We wrestle to establish power in our jobs, our communities and our families. We negotiate for the best deals in our relationships, whether personal, casual or professional. Then, at the end of the day, if we have not encountered sufficient drama, we turn on the television or surf the Internet for an extra fix.

Many popular teachings place great value on obstacles and all manner of adversity, even illness. Because they are seen as opportunities for learning, growth and personal development, challenges are welcomed, even sought out; they are believed to be essential for earning a share of that elusive infinite abundance and a sense of self-satisfaction. When the going gets tough, the tough get going. It's not how many times you fall but how many times you get back up. What doesn't kill you will make you stronger. It's not the destination that matters; it's the journey. These are trendy sayings commonly used as prods by trainers and coaches. With each small victory, we derive self-validation, pride, satisfaction, strength, confidence and the willingness to continue to forge ahead and face a new day, and then again, a new battle. And on and on go the battles in the stories of our lives.

Our long-standing appreciation for—and fascination with—life's challenges leaves us with a rather compelling, if not altogether disturbing, conclusion: peace and harmony will appear unsatisfactory, even boring, and so will be less inviting than conflict, struggle and even hardship. That being the case, in most encounters and endeavours, the experience of peace is not likely to be the first choice. Even if at times frightening and unsettling, in the face of possible victory and the satisfaction it promises, drama is much more attractive than peace. In an interview with Bill Moyers, renowned mythologist Joseph Campbell expressed this well: "The writer must be true to truth. And that's a killer because the only way you can describe a human being truly is by describing his imperfections. The perfect human being is uninteresting—the Buddha who leaves the world… It is the imperfections of life that are lovable." While this view may once upon a time have been tolerable, even acceptable, one might ask if it is still relevant today. Is this really how we want to measure our worth? How much longer must we remain bound to seeking out and overcoming our imperfections?

Of all the stories we tell ourselves and share with others, at the end of the day, the most important story is the one we believe. Whether we are conscious of it or not, our beliefs colour all of our actions, motivations and responses to life. However, as important as they are, we rarely stop to question our beliefs; in fact, we are taught that to question beliefs is to show a lack of faith. What is not understood is that beliefs are like scaffolding; they are merely temporary structures that can be leaned on while construction is underway. Like scaffolding, beliefs can limit or even block the view. Essentially, beliefs serve only to support us while we shift to a new level of knowing. There comes a time when, as with scaffolding, beliefs must be abandoned so that a new way of seeing and being can be embraced and experienced. Perhaps it is time to question how it is that we are faced with never-ending battles, that we are destined to suffer loss, sickness and death while we exist in the middle of an infinite universe. We might begin to wonder if we are missing something, if we are capable of experiencing more. What would happen if we abandoned our beliefs and opened ourselves to a new story?

In Search of a Better Story

On an individual level, few would challenge the fact that their life began at a point in time referred to as physical birth, and that this same life will end in an experience of physical death. One need not have attended a great number of births and funerals to accept this as unquestionable fact. Life is sometimes good, maybe very good, yet it remains fraught with the constant meeting of needs, the overcoming of obstacles, loss, pain, suffering, challenges and, ultimately, death. It is usually not until circumstances have become unbearable through sickness or tragedy that the birth-life-death cycle comes into question.

Our teachings hold that the Source of Life is infinite, perfect and whole and that we are created in the image of this Source. Many people wholeheartedly accept these teachings as truth. Yet, infinity, perfection and wholeness continue to elude us. As humanity reaches for a greater experience of conscious awareness, some are beginning to question, even challenge, our traditional stories of creation. If we exist in the middle of an infinite universe, formed by boundless, continually renewing life energies, it makes sense that this infinite flow of life would be part of our experience.

There is little doubt that the heart of humanity is stirring. Faced with a growing sense of dissatisfaction with life, an increasing number of men and women of all ages are expressing their desire for a different way of being in the world. Many souls are disillusioned with the current state of the world; they are growing hungry for an experience of wholeness, healing, peace, harmony, lasting joy and fulfilment. They are searching for something more relevant and more satisfying than what can be found in ancient and traditional religious, mystical and spiritual teachings. In answer to the need for a perspective that can provide clarity and healing in all aspects of our everyday lives, from the spiritual to the mundane, new teachings are emerging. Some of these teachings are proposing answers for those previously unanswerable questions, some even promising the attainment of that once lofty, intangible goal—enlightenment.

It was not so long ago that discourses on awakening, ascension, enlightenment, holiness, cosmic consciousness, conscious awareness or infinite awareness were reserved for gurus, masters, priests, initiates, theologians, theosophists and metaphysicians. Enlightenment, or awakening, was considered to be a lofty goal to be attained by a select, deserving few who had devoted their lives to the purification of their souls through disciplined, sometimes secret, even painful, practices, usually under the tutelage of an "enlightened" master or guru. Only after successful completion of the most demanding of tasks would the deserving student be worthy of consideration for ascension to the higher realms. Although they may once have been helpful for some seekers, and may still be suitable for a few, such paths are likely to hold little appeal for the questioning mind in dire need of immediate clarification for situations and conditions arising in a world of increasing complexity, stress and confusion.

Unable to relate in a satisfactory manner to any spiritual, religious or New Age teaching, with the thought of God on the back burner, many will simply dedicate themselves to making the best of the human condition. Attention and effort are placed on developing and maintaining a life of relative comfort and ease while adapting, and often yielding, to changing socio-economic trends. The common approach for those who hold no spiritual aspirations is to grow up and make it to adulthood as painlessly as possible. They will work hard to acquire the skills needed to function in the world with an acceptable level of satisfaction, happiness and accomplishment, grow old with as little discomfort as possible and eventually come face-to-face with the inevitable—death. If they have lived a good life, paid their dues, maybe given back to the community, it's been a good life. Sufficiently busy with the everyday stuff of life, they will seldom wonder if there might be something beyond this cycle of birth, survival, perhaps a comfortable and productive life, aging and, inevitably, death. When life is very good, or even passably okay, there is little reason to question the nature of reality.

Dissatisfied because God has not stepped in to correct the ills of humanity or, more importantly, disheartened because He has not been there in their times of need, others will deliberately avoid all things religious or spiritual. Atheism seems to be the most sensible alternative. Better to have no God at all than to blindly accept a God whose existence is impossible to prove or, worse, a God who does not seem to care about His creations. How could a loving God allow a single child to suffer for even an instant? Scientists tell us that the source of life is a big bang, the cause of which remains a mystery, but they are confident that one day, with sufficient funding for their research or with more sophisticated tools to work with, they will have the answer. We'll wait and see what they will reveal next.

For a growing number of individuals, especially the young, none of these ways of looking at life are acceptable. Judged as troublesome malcontents, they may be scolded or shunned for their relentless questioning or punished for their stubborn refusal to accept things as they are. Baffled by their aberrant behaviour, distraught parents wonder where they went wrong. "That's just the way life is," pleads the desperate parent. "Try to get used to it. You'll understand when you're older." But something deep inside these troubled youth—a still, small voice—refuses to accept this limited, and decidedly hopeless, view of life. Who wants to grow up, become a productive member of society—a society that doesn't understand you and probably doesn't even give a damn about you—only to end up in a coffin? They are the misfits, the ones for whom adequate answers are nowhere to be found, those who are most likely to seek release through various forms of distractions and addictions such as drugs, games, work or whatever form of mind-numbing activity keeps the questions and the discomfort at bay.

Fuelled by an unrelenting desire to know the truth, a small number will turn this unrest into an active search for answers. Out of desperation, a few of these struggling souls will find their way to my office; when appropriate, I may point out that their discomfort with the way things are might be a good thing. In fact, to question currently accepted limited beliefs may be a sign of sanity, an indication that the Soul—that still, small voice buried deep within—is reaching out and seeking to be heard, but more than that, it is requiring much more of life. There must be another way, they say, to which I reply, yes, perhaps there is.

> Is this a LITTLE Voice, so small and still It cannot rise above the senseless noise of sounds that have no meaning? God willed not His Son forget Him. And the power of His Will is in the Voice that speaks for Him. (ACIM, Chap. 31, p. 703)

Releasing the Fear of God

Motivated by the paralyzing fear of my early French-Canadian Catholic education, at a young age I decided that I had better be very, very good; the threat of the purges of purgatory or worse—the horrors of hell—were enough to keep me in line. The God of my childhood seemed more capricious than benevolent; He was judgmental, punishing, vengeful and frightening. I also found it very difficult to understand how He could have favourites. Why would

He hold a place in Heaven for Catholics while everyone else would end up in purgatory or, worse, hell? Admittedly, He was not a very approachable God. He was a God that you might want to avoid, just in case you had unknowingly committed some unpardonable sin.

I also learned that only priests had the privilege of speaking directly with God, which made me resent having been born a girl since the priesthood was not an option open to women in the Catholic faith. The rest of us mere mortals were taught to pray to God and ask for forgiveness, although I never did quite understand what I had done that required asking for forgiveness. We were limited to a one-way conversation: pray for forgiveness but don't expect that God will answer you. We were to confess our sins to the priests, and the priests would speak to God on our behalf. It certainly never occurred to me to talk to God directly. From that perspective, I found myself at the foot of the ladder to Heaven, with no hope of ever reaching the top, in a world created by a God that I could never reach, let alone one with whom I could commune. Being the obedient Catholic girl that I was, no doubt having misunderstood the teachings of the Church and probably confused beyond any hope of understanding, like many, I didn't give the subject further thought until much later in life.

Many people are skittish about the word "God." Up until the age of fifty, I never would have imagined myself writing about God, never, *ever*. It is only in recent years that I discovered that to talk about God as a benevolent, loving Father or Mother, or even to talk to God directly, is normal for many Christians as well as for people of other faiths. It took a major leap of faith on my part to embrace a different view of the nature and meaning of God. It required the release of most of my beliefs before I could accept the radical possibility that God is the creator of all, including me, that God is good and He will hear and, more importantly, answer if only I dare to speak with and listen to Him. The acceptance of this new perspective has brought greater rewards than a lifetime of prayer and study could ever have brought because it has made God real and, most of all, accessible.

So, how does one talk about God without actually talking about God? After writing four books on my journey with *A Course in Miracles*, a work in which God is mentioned over 2,200 times, one might wonder why this might have been a problem. In over thirty years of consultation practice, I rarely, if ever, brought up anything to do with God. Working with people of all ages, from diverse cultural, spiritual and religious backgrounds—mostly non-practising—I learned to work around the subject and use language and metaphors that were suitable for my clients.

Given my initial lack of connection with God, whenever I needed to refer to something of a "higher" order, it was easy to go along with the popular trend of replacing the word "God" with more approachable and non-spiritual ones such as the Universe, Infinite Energy, the Eternal or the Source of all Life. The use of language that causes the least amount of discomfort and evokes the greatest degree of trust, safety and hope makes it easier to establish a connection with this Source. Although I did come to appreciate the words "God" and "Father," even "Mother," for their warm, accessible sense, not wanting to come across as a crazed God-lover, I continued to use language that was appropriate for my clients. I kept my burgeoning relationship with the Father private, and so I became a closeted lover of God.

Despite having made peace with God, I delayed working on this book for months. Actually, by the time I hit the keyboard, more than a year had passed. How does one talk about God without talking about God, I wondered. Then one morning, a simple answer came: by redefining God. It is not so much the existence of a God that is the issue but rather our current understanding—our misconceptions—of what or who God is. What is needed is a new definition, one that speaks to today's seeker.

Shortly afterwards, the strangest thing happened—or perhaps not so strange for those who understand how things work when we begin to connect with our Source. Over the weeks that followed that little bit of insight, a significant number of my clients brought up the subject of God during consultations, and this occurred with no prompting on my part. From the Syrian taxi driver who talked about how he loved to sit in churches so he could be close to God, to the concerned mother of teens who placed their welfare in His hands, they shared their struggles with outdated beliefs and their sincere desire for a more intimate experience of God. With their questions, they effectively invited me out of my closet; I thanked the Father for letting me know that it was time to talk about God. And if I needed a further sign, *The Story of God*, a documentary series narrated by Morgan Freeman, one of my favourite actors, was announced on the National Geographic Channel. I needed no further prompting; it was time to talk about God.

What is interesting about this new trend of openness to God among my clients is that hardly any were students of *A Course in Miracles* and only a very few were pursuing an active spiritual path. Clearly there exists a desire for a greater experience of our humanity that stems from a powerful force deep within each individual, and this desire is being expressed regardless of whether or not a person is a spiritual seeker.

A New Story of God

When addressing questions about the meaning of existence and the origin of life, we almost invariably encounter the subject of God. Most people today have been exposed to a teaching, usually in the form of a myth that describes the origins of the universe, the world and humanity. Though a popular way of transmitting teachings, myths remain made-up stories that are shaped and coloured by beliefs that may or may not have their foundation in reality. They are then passed down to future generations, at which time these beliefs may no longer be relevant and may need to be re-examined.

Many of us have been taught that an all-powerful, all-knowing, almighty Being, or God, created all things in heaven and earth, and from a mystical, unreachable place above, He continues to oversee His creation. As lowly, even unworthy, insignificant mortals, we should be content with any amount of good He deigns to send our way. Some will take these teachings literally, without question, while others will simply forget about them, not finding any practical purpose for them in their lives.

The well-known story of Adam and Eve depicts how the first man came to this world. After having created the world, God created Adam, the first human, and from his rib, He created Eve, a companion for Adam. They were given a lovely garden in which to live, a paradise where all of their needs were met. However, a bit too curious for her own good, Eve convinced Adam that it might be okay to eat the one fruit that had been forbidden. Experiencing guilt for the first time and then fearful of the consequences of their insubordination, they ran for cover. As feared, upon learning of their disobedience, God chased them down and banished them from the Garden of Eden as just punishment. In this story, the human condition is portrayed as having been founded on sin, guilt and fear. This story portrays God as unforgiving and unloving, a father who knowingly sets a trap for his children. The belief in man's inherently sinful nature remains unchallenged by millions of people today.

The traditional portrayal of God as an all-powerful, all-knowing yet judgmental, vengeful and wrathful deity seems more human than divine in origin. In fact, this God appears to be the product of overactive human imagination. Such a view is no doubt founded on fear and long-standing ignorance rather than on an inspired sense of a loving, divine Presence or a knowing that only direct experience can offer. Not surprisingly, some inquisitive souls are beginning to question how an all-knowing, infinite, perfect, loving God could create beings that are defective from the start, tainted by sin, fraught with the never-ending meeting of needs, destined to suffer loss, sickness and death. If God creates like Himself, as some teachings claim, it does not make sense that He created both good and evil, love and hate, wholeness and illness, light and darkness, life and death. Such polarizations would inhibit the harmonious flow of life, and so cannot be expressions of an infinite Source of Life.

This kind of God certainly does not inspire faith or trust, so it is no wonder that attendance in traditional churches and places of worship is waning. Many New Age and self-help teachings simply avoid the subject of God, using more neutral terms such as "universe," "spirit," "abundance" or "energy" instead. Although this approach can be helpful, it tends to be somewhat intellectual and may fail to foster the establishment of a close, personal, interactive relationship with the Source. A safe, intimate communion with an approachable, loving Source or a caring Father or Mother figure will make it easier to open up to the knowing that lies beyond what can be derived from intellect alone: it will promote a readiness to experience what God is being in the moment.

A Course in Miracles sheds light on the dilemma of God by stating that God is in all things; God is forever being, moving, expressing Himself, Herself or Itself every moment in all things, including you and me, right here, right now. That which is infinite cannot be bound by a timeline; therefore, it cannot have a beginning, a middle or an end. It follows that only the present moment—here, now—is real. Infinite Mind exists in the present moment, and since It is infinite, It must forever be being something new, in every moment.

If God is creating all things like Himself in each moment, then He cannot be separate from His creations, and all of His creations must be contained in Him. If He is in all things, then everything that is expressed has its source in the One Mind, the Mind of God. Since our Source—God, Father/Mother or Infinite Mind—encompasses all things, It cannot create evil or anything that would cause hurt or the destruction of any of Its creations, great or small. It follows that the substance of God must be Love, for Love is all-inclusive. This perspective offers a more appealing way of seeing and approaching God, one that may allow us to release some long-held, no longer suitable, beliefs.

> Oneness is simply the idea God is. And in His Being, He encompasses all things. No mind holds anything but Him. We say "God is," and then we cease to speak, for in that knowledge words are meaningless. (ACIM, Lesson 169)

Talking to God

I suppose now that I am out of the closet I can relate this little story. I had gotten into the habit of joining with God at night before going to bed and in the morning before getting involved in the day's business. Above all else, I would remind myself, I want to be in the presence of God; I want to know more of what is available to be experienced. *Father, here I am; I'm here to serve.* One morning, as I prepared for the day, I asked, *Where would you like me to be today, Father?* And then, clearly, as though spoken by someone standing next to my bed, I heard the words, *With me.* Overwhelmed by the sense of the loving Presence that was with me at that moment, tears rolled from my sleepy eyes. I understood that I was to be more conscious about choosing to be in the presence of God throughout the day—and what a glorious day it was. I also understood that this should be the goal and sole purpose of every day—of every moment of every day. Seek only to be in the presence of God—the loving, infinite Source, Mother, Father, the One Mind—and all things will be made clear. This is the only worthwhile goal. It is that simple.

While I was finishing the first draft of this chapter and reviewing what I had shared about God, I realized that I was still seeing God as God and me as me. I still saw myself as something separate from God; I was not experiencing the Oneness I was seeking. If there is no God "out there," if God is being All in All, who had spoken to me that day in answer to my prayer? Was I going nuts?

In answer to these questions, my Friend explained that I should not worry, that, even if there is no individuality or personality per se, God will speak to us in the way that is most appropriate for our present need. Whether we call It God, Father/Mother, Source, One Mind, Infinite Energy, Eternal Life Principle or Divine Intelligence, our prayer will be answered because the true nature of the Source of Life is Love, and Love will never turn down a call for help.

In the Presence of God

It was early June when I finally got to work on this book. It had been a long winter, and so the greening of the leaves and the blossoming of the lilacs and other spring-blooming trees was a most welcome sight. One morning, I woke up to see the rays of the sun cutting through the blinds of my bedroom window. *Wow*, I thought, as I engaged in my waking ritual of being in the presence of God. *What a glorious day.* Absorbed in the awesomeness and the beauty of nature, I was moved by my part in being aware of it. I wanted to know more of what God was being in everything and everyone around me.

The following morning, I woke up to the patter of rain on my bedroom window. *Wow*, I thought, as I joined with God, *what a glorious day*, once again overwhelmed with the joy of belonging to something so awesome. I laughed when I realized I had had the same reaction the day before but under opposite weather conditions. At that moment, I knew that as a tiny expression of the Infinite Movement of Life, my function was simply to appreciate all aspects of creation, great or small. Would these non-events make for a good story? Not likely. Would I trade these moments for any amount of worldly glory? No! To be in the presence of God and to see God in everything surpasses all other forms of reward and, more importantly, it is the path to another way of being in the world.

> How instantly the memory of God arises in the mind that has no fear to keep the memory away. (ACIM, Chap. 28, p. 648)

CHAPTER 2

The Story of Man

The world you see is an illusion of a world. God did not create it, for what He creates must be eternal as Himself. (ACIM, Preface, p. ix)

The Agreement

If there is a Source, which we may call God, Father/Mother, Oneness, Eternal Life or Infinite Mind, and Its nature is whole, all-inclusive, perfect and forever being new, and if what the Source creates is like Itself, we will need to reconsider this very real, finite, imperfect, disorderly world in which we appear to live. If this is true, it must then follow that sickness, imperfection, death—in fact, limitation of any kind—cannot exist, yet from our perspective, they do exist. *A Course in Miracles* explains that the problem lies in the mistaken assumption that our experience as beings residing in bodies is all there is to us. If we are not experiencing the infinite nature of life, we are simply experiencing a distorted perception of Reality.

If existence apart from the Source is not possible, what did happen? Very simply, the Course tells us, nothing happened; that is, nothing that could have an actual impact on Reality. If everything that exists is an ongoing expression of the all-encompassing Mind of God, the Source of all life whose nature is perfect Oneness, then nothing can exist outside or apart from It. Since we cannot be separate from our Source, our apparent existence as separate, independent, self-directed individuals can only be imaginary. By all appearances, we are living in a world of our making in which we can pretend to be what we are not. While God is creating life in perfect harmony, beauty and wholeness, we are making up our own version of reality. The world we see is not the world as God is *being* it at the moment; it is simply the world we wish to have, a world that is a product of our collective imagination.

Admittedly, we have done an excellent job of convincing ourselves that there could be a way of living outside the realm of Reality, something we have come to know as the world, our universe. But, this made-up world exists only as long as we maintain the belief that it is possible to function independently from our Source, from the Father/Mother, the One Mind. It is the belief that fosters the state of duality: darkness versus light, good versus evil, life versus death, self versus non-self, and it is essentially a denial of our Oneness with All. While such an imaginary experience can seem so utterly real, in truth, it can never be real nor can it have any effect on Reality. But how can the world not be real when everything in our experience proves to us that it is very real? No one in his or her right mind would attempt to deny the existence of the world, or would they? Might not such an attempt at denial be considered cause for concern or, worse, evidence of insanity? Our individual, firsthand, undeniable experience validates the world.

In our experience, the world exists because we can touch it, taste it, smell it, see it, hear it. But do these sensory experiences constitute the entirety of our potential for experiencing reality? What about mind, knowing, intuition, consciousness, inspiration, creativity, feeling, sensing and love? These are not sensory experiences, and although they may seem to stem from them, or may appear to be in some way related, they are in fact beyond sensory experience. If we base the existence of the world on sensory data alone, our definition is likely to be incomplete, perhaps even inaccurate. If our experience has thus far been limited, what more is there to be experienced? What keeps us bound to this incomplete way of being?

So it is that our cherished life stories, which reflect our current beliefs, are describing what *might* happen if the sons and daughters of God, expressions of the Infinite Life Source, were to pretend to be separate from their Source. *A Course in Miracles* explains that if we are experiencing a limitation on our divinity, it is because we have chosen—and continue to choose—to have this limited experience. We have agreed among ourselves to define the parameters of a made-up world, and we are defining our experience based on the belief that it is possible to exist separate and apart from our Source. This is the essential mistaken belief that is at the root of the human condition. We are collectively sustaining our version of reality in order to enjoy an experience of independence from Perfect Oneness; truly, this is a form of collective insanity.

The world of our making is cleverly designed to convince us that we have accomplished the impossible: separation from the Source of all Life, from the One Mind. Everything we currently know about the world serves to uphold the belief that we are independent beings, existing in material forms that we call bodies, and that our lives depend on the healthy functioning and protection of these bodies. We have completely forgotten that we are essentially thought expressions of the Infinite Mind—we are Mind, not merely bodies. We experience the world and our universe as matter rather than mind because matter serves to limit and circumscribe, thereby establishing the illusion that people and things are distinct and undeniably separate from each other. As long as we continue to cling to our current beliefs about the nature of the world, from inanimate objects to human biology, we are excluding from our experience the eternal flowing movement and subtler meanings of creation, in particular the Love that is its nature.

The vastness and complexity of the world in which we appear to live is a testament to the power of the human mind and, above all, human will. We liberally make use of the term "creating" for what man is making, but that would be giving creative power to man, a power that is only available to the true Source of Life. Since man does not have the power to alter what God is creating, "making" is a better term for what man expresses while in the human condition. As long as we remain unaware of the illusory nature of our limited, independent human experience, we continue to derive great pride in our accomplishments and "creations" in the world, especially in recent years with all manner of manufacturing, technological and scientific progress. However, as long as these expressions are not sourced in Love and a sense of the Oneness of humanity and all of creation, they are not God-derived and can have no real impact in Reality. Only that which is joined with its Source can express true creative power.

> YOU are the dreamer of the world of dreams. No other cause it has, nor ever will. Nothing more fearful than an idle dream has terrified God's Son, and made him think that he has lost his innocence, denied his Father, and made war upon himself.... God willed he waken gently, and with joy. And gave him means to waken without fear. Accept the dream He gave instead of yours. It is not difficult to change a dream when once the dreamer has been recognized. (ACIM, Chap. 27, p. 640)

Our experience can be likened to that of a group of young children who, early one rainy morning, decide to exercise their imaginations by heading down to the playroom to create a fantasy world in which to play games of "let's pretend." If we were to peek into the playroom, we might find that a few chairs have been moved around so a schoolteacher can properly address her students or that an empty box has been converted into a spaceship for those intrepid space travellers seeking out alien life forms. Absorbed in their make-believe world, the morning hours pass and the youngsters completely forget where they are, even missing their mother's call to come upstairs for lunch.

Meanwhile, Mother does not accuse them of sin or wrongdoing of any kind; she simply calls again. If they still don't answer, she may send an older brother to remind them that it is time to put aside their games and join the others for a bowl of hot soup and a grilled cheese sandwich. Wishing to delay the inevitable return to the "real" world just a little while longer, the youngsters might draw the older sibling into their fantasy so that he may be assigned the role of disruptive student interrupting the class, or dangerous alien from outer space. Still, Mother will not punish her children. She loves them, and she knows they are safe; they have simply become wrapped up in their imaginary games. Eventually, they will return upstairs to enjoy the sunshine that is piercing through the thinning clouds.

Similarly, as adventurous children of God, we have come together and agreed to make up a world of our own, one that is separate from our Source, so that what we are experiencing is a dream or fantasy world. The world of form as we perceive it is sustained only by an agreement held between a group of brothers and sisters, expressions of the Infinite Life Source, who have decided to play a game of separation, to experience self-sustaining autonomy and independence. Awareness of this agreement is essential not only for an understanding of the current human condition, which is little more than a daydream, but also because it provides an important key to our release or our awakening from the dream. For this game of pretend to work, there must be two or more who have agreed to imagine a world apart from God, separate from our Source. As we choose to experience our true wholeness and we begin to withdraw from the game of separation, we contribute to the healing of all of humanity. If there are no players, there can be no game.

> You are at home in God, dreaming of exile, but perfectly capable of awakening to reality. Is it your will to do so? You know, from your own experience, that what you see in dreams you think is real as long as you are asleep. Yet the instant you waken you KNOW that everything that SEEMED to happen did not happen at all. You do not think this mysterious, even though all the laws of what you awakened TO were violated while you slept. Is it not possible that you merely shifted from one dream to another, without REALLY wakening? (ACIM, Chap. 9, p. 221)

The Kingdom of the Ego

That part of us that chooses to believe in and maintain the idea of a life separate from the Infinite Life Source is what *A Course in Miracles* refers to as the ego, the character in a game of pretend. Since this "ego sense of self" is made up, that is, it does not have its source in the Infinite Mind, it is not and can never be real.

Because the ego is not sourced in Infinity, tremendous energy must be expended for it to be sustained. Still, the ego has no true power of its own. While we engage in the ego's version of life, it is as though we are attempting to stop the movement of creation to take control of the flow of life, like pressing the pause button on the remote control while watching a movie so we can imagine a scenario of our choosing. The ego sense of self brings the natural flow of life to a halt and makes up its own scenarios.

The dream world, or the world of separation from Source, is the kingdom of the ego. It is a world in which we seem to be faced with what appear to be very real needs, from food and clothing to shelter. Since separation is not natural, we must constantly work at protecting ourselves against threats to our survival, all of which are imaginary, since that which has its source in the Infinite Mind cannot be vulnerable. As long as we identify with the ego sense of self, as thinking beings that reside in bodies, we boldly, courageously, even heroically, set out to meet these needs and face down the threats to our survival.

We cling to, even vigorously defend, our beliefs about ourselves and about how the universe works, but our beliefs serve only to sustain and reinforce the ego sense of ourselves. While we maintain this limited experience, we hold the movement of life hostage so we can indulge in our desire for autonomy a little while longer. We wilfully, even happily, assume responsibility for our lives, something that is impossible because we can never be responsible for Life. We can only pretend to be in charge of our lives, to play at being masters of our destinies, all of which is occurring in a make-believe world. As long as we continue to experience life from within bodies, through physical senses, as separate beings, independent from one another, unaware of the interconnectedness of All that is, we will continue to believe that we have successfully broken free from our Source and fear will hover at the edges of our awareness. From this perspective, we cannot know complete satisfaction, healing, fulfilment, joy, peace or love. It is our ill-founded beliefs that interfere with an experience of infinite knowing, a knowing that has always been available to us and remains available every minute of every day.

> The body's serial adventures, from the time of birth to dying is the theme of every dream the world has ever had. The "hero" of this dream will never change, nor will its purpose. Though the dream itself takes many forms, and seems to show a great variety of places and events wherein its "hero" finds itself, the dream has but one purpose, taught in many ways. This single lesson does it try to teach again, and still again, and yet once more; that it is CAUSE and NOT effect. And YOU are its effect, and CANNOT be its cause. (ACIM, Chap. 27, p. 641)

While many believe that struggle is good, the need for struggle is unnecessary, a fabrication of the ego. It says I am imperfect, I am defective, I am unworthy, I must work hard to become something, to be someone. This is the story of my life. This happened to me in my childhood, it's not really my fault; my parents taught me to behave this way; I was influenced by my culture; I have been conditioned by society. I am a victim of (insert your favourite story about yourself here), and that is why I am the way I am. Just ask my therapist; there is a name for my disorder. Our beliefs also extend to our physical health: it's normal to feel this way at my age; I suffer from a chronic condition; I have a genetic mutation; my illness is terminal, the doctors have said there is nothing more they can do.

This view of incompleteness and vulnerability is based on the ego sense of self. It is founded on a fantasy version of life chosen and maintained in order to sustain the illusion of a life separate from the Source of all Life. The truth is that we are perfect, we are whole and the need for struggle is ill-founded because nothing can exist apart from perfect Oneness. All we need is to allow the good in us to flow freely so we can become everything that we truly are as expressions of a perfect, divine, loving Life Source.

Since separation is not possible, it is a false state and will always be at risk of being revealed for what it is—a product of the imagination. That which is not real can never truly feel comfortable and safe, and, as such, can only foster a sense of vulnerability and a need for defensiveness. The ego sense of self is always in danger since its very existence is pure fabrication, and it can be extinguished in an instant. Since the outcome of awakening is the disintegration of illusions due to their abandonment, in the face of an unknown of this magnitude, at least as perceived from within the dream state, resistance and fear are bound to be encountered.

We applaud our heroes, our thinkers, our scientists for their great contributions to the world, a dream world. We venerate our heroes because, according to our myths, they are the ones who will save us from threats to our very existence. We project onto these special men and women the responsibility of saving us from something that is entirely our responsibility, our decision for vulnerability, our rejection of our infinite nature as expressions of the Infinite Mind. When our heroes fail in their mighty task, we find a way to crucify them. Meanwhile, the only thing that we need to be saved from is our mistaken choice, our decision to live in a way that is incomplete, separate from the Source, therefore, not sane. We are the hero, a make-believe character, in our story, and the outcome of our story depends on the choices made by this character.

A Tiny, Mad Idea

So here we are, apparently experiencing a deep sleep in which we are having dreams, some of us enjoying good dreams, even great dreams, while others are suffering nightmares, yet all of it so convincingly real. Why have we come together and agreed to make up a world of our own that is separate from our Source, a world that is clearly far from perfect, a world of struggle and strife, just to have the whole thing end up with death, likely preceded by some form of debilitating disease? Why do we continue to agree to have this limited experience of life if it is our nature—our birthright, our natural inheritance as expressions of the Infinite Life Source, as sons and daughters of God—to experience infinity? If God is All there is, being All in All, how is it that we are experiencing something that is clearly not God-like, a world of pain, sorrow, lack and suffering for far too many of our brothers and sisters?

The answer is that we made up this world because we have the ability to do so. We have simply chosen to pretend to be separate from our Source and to live in a made-up world because we *can*. It is what *A Course in Miracles* refers to as a "tiny, mad idea," nothing real, nothing of any consequence. We are essentially free to choose our experience and, given our innate curiosity about life and ourselves, we have exercised this freedom with wild abandon. While exercising our freedom, we have become so engrossed in the experience that we have completely forgotten our true heritage. We are like the group of children who are playing in the basement and have become so involved in make-believe games that they have forgotten that they could go outside and enjoy a much larger playground.

> You do not realize how much you have denied yourself, and how much God, in His Love, would not have it so. Yet He would not interfere with you because He would not know His Son if he were not free. To interfere with you would be to attack Himself, and God is not insane. When you denied Him, YOU were insane. (ACIM, Chap. 9, p. 230)

But, we ask with haughty indignation, if there is a God, a loving Father, and if He is all-knowing, how could He let His children choose for anything less than their divine birthright? How could a loving Mother allow her children to experience one instant of suffering? The Infinite Intelligence, our Source, Creator, Father/Mother will not interfere with our freedom to choose our experience because freedom is part of our essential nature. Our ability to choose is an aspect of the ongoing creative movement of Life of which we are an integral part and from which we could never be separate.

The dream state, which is nothing more than ignorance of our true divine nature, has not been imposed on us. The human condition is not a form of punishment for our sins, it is not and has never been a requirement for our growth and learning, nor are we in any way bound to uphold it, improve it, fix it or continue to experience it. We are free to choose to play a little longer and remain in our limited make-believe daydream for as long as we desire, or we can simply choose to abandon the game and experience our true reality as expressions of an infinite, loving Life Source.

However, while we have the ability and the freedom to choose to dream up a complex fantasy and to experience a substitute for Reality, we do not have the ability or the power to create anything real or to alter Reality. True creative energy is available to us only when we are experiencing our Oneness, when we are joined with the Infinite Life Source. That being the case, there is no need for a Divine Power to step in and save us or interfere in any way with our choice. Nor will we be punished for our decision to daydream for a while, since it has no real effect. How could we have left Reality, the Kingdom of Heaven, if there exists no other place *but* Reality? There cannot *be* any place outside of perfect Oneness.

If we are collectively choosing how we are living in our dream world, from the perspective of individual, separate selves, this isn't looking good for humanity, especially when we consider the ongoing conflict, divisiveness, disharmony and hardship experienced by far too many of our brothers and sisters. Many believe that humanity is undergoing a normal, even accelerated process of evolution, that we are better off now than we were thousands or even hundreds of years ago. Once again, since what the Source creates is like Itself, whole and perfect, we must be inherently whole. The idea of evolution can only belong to the fantasy version of reality; it is simply the evolution of a storyline in a daydream we are exploring. It seems to exist so long as we value our separate existence and desire to delay the experience of the Oneness of creation. It is a concept devised by dreaming children and serves to prevent sudden awakening by prolonging the dream experience.

Any process of evolution and growth is therefore not necessary and remains a construct of the separated illusory self. This way of seeing life is an invention of the ego. It is only the ego that can appreciate struggle and hardship because the overcoming of obstacles gives it a sense of purpose, a definition, a sense of accomplishment. Central to the concept of evolution is the assumption that all is occurring in time; this fosters the belief that healing and awakening will take time. However, healing of mind and body can be instantaneous once we realize that illness is simply the temporary absence of wholeness, that we have simply replaced wholeness with a belief in limitation and incompleteness.

Awakening can happen in an instant when we decide that we no longer wish to experience illusion and limitation of any kind. Since our dream is being experienced in the middle of Reality, the only alternative is to wake up so that we may then have a full experience of Reality. While we are busily engaged in our fascinating little fantasies, Life is being expressed around, in and through us. It is an experience of wholeness, uninterrupted fulfillment and joy that is our birthright as expressions of the Infinite Life Source. It is this experience of a complete Life that awakening will uncover.

One day, I shared with my guide that I was feeling confused and pulled between what felt like two distinct worlds: the limited world of the ego and a new world of infinite possibilities. My Friend helped me understand what I was experiencing. "There are not two worlds, there is only one world, and it is seen either clearly or through the filters of an illusory experience, through the lens of the ego sense of self. No effort is required to see clearly. All you need is to relinquish your hold on the limited perception. What is tiring and exhausting is to cling to the small, dense experience to which you have applied your own meanings.

"Waking up goes against everything that the ego deems to be reasonable, intelligent, valuable, important and acceptable. If you feel that the new direction that you are taking is uncomfortable, maybe even awkward, or perhaps it may even seem that you are going in the opposite direction to that with which you are familiar, you may take this as a good sign. It simply means that you are moving away from the ego sense of self toward your divine Self, toward more of what you really are. When feeling that you are going to miss something once you awaken, remember that only the ego can miss anything. In Reality, nothing can be missed. Everything is One. There cannot be any longing in Reality. Besides, all that the ego longs for and is afraid it will miss is not real.

> "Although fear or a sense of loss or resistance may be encountered, it does not mean that you are doing anything wrong—quite the contrary. It is an indication that you are breaking loose from the hold or the clutches of the ego. You do not need to go any faster than is comfortable. This feeling of loss is not an indicator of failure. You are experiencing a period of adjustment. That's all. Nor is it surprising or unusual to have this experience given that being on the path toward Home marks the end of the ego sense of self, that with which you have been familiar for such a long time."

> Illusions will not last. Their death is sure, and this alone is certain in their world. It is the ego's world because of this. What is the ego? But a dream of what you really are. A thought you are apart from your Creator and a wish to be what He created not. It is a thing of madness, not reality at all. A name for namelessness is all it is. A symbol of impossibility; a choice for options that do not exist. (ACIM, Preface, p. vi)

Capable of So Much More

I was sitting on the balcony one afternoon, enjoying the beauty of the flowers blooming in the pots next to my chair. Music poured out through the patio door from the classical station I had tuned it to that morning. I had been feeling troubled by the current state of humanity, wondering how it was that humanity could have gone so far astray while nature seemed to express such beauty. Why did a begonia seem to express so much more intelligence than humanity? I shifted my attention to the music; it was one of my favourite pieces, Rachmaninoff's 2nd Piano Concerto. At that moment, an answer came in response to my expression of distress. Tears rolled down my cheeks as I realized that yes, we are capable of so much more. When this wonderful musical creation ended, the fourth movement of Beethoven's 9th Symphony took its place; I cried some more. Yes, I realized with a deep sigh of relief, humanity is capable of so much more, and we have indeed expressed much beauty.

CHAPTER 3

Waking Up to Reality

To think that God made chaos, contradicts His Will, invented opposites to truth, and suffers death to triumph over life; all this is arrogance. Humility would see at once these things are not of Him. And can you see what God created not? To think you can is merely to believe you can perceive what God willed not to be. And what could be more arrogant than this? (ACIM, Lesson 152)

Armageddon Demystified

As an inquisitive youth growing up in the fifties and sixties, I searched for answers in books. I must admit that I had strange interests as a teen, being more curious about the afterlife and the meaning of existence than I was about just being a normal teen. In fact, I couldn't even tell you what "normal" teens were into in those days. Since this was the pre-Internet era, my search was confined to books in print format, starting with officially authorized spiritual publications, and a mixed bag of works from Darwin to Dickens. I say "officially authorized" because for a number of years I only read books that bore the seal of approval of the Church. I was a good Catholic, or better yet, a frightened Catholic, so I guess that made me a good Catholic in the eyes of the Church, at least until I dared to explore outside the library of permitted literature.

Today's seeker, young or old, has access to a constantly growing library of information in a variety of formats from the written word to a vast array of audiovisual materials, covering everything from fantasy to science. Had I been born a half-century later, I don't know how I would have fared in the face of this overwhelming amount of data. Since normalcy is measured by the ability to adapt to current standards, knowing myself, I suspect that, like many unsettled young people, I probably would not have fared all that well. Today, I can fully sympathize with those young millennials who find it difficult to accept what they see as a world of chaos and inequality.

Our brains all function a little differently. Some resonate well with stories, and others do better with pure theory and abstraction. I like stories; show me how you did it so I can learn from your experience. But, having a linear thinking mind, I tend to take things literally, and so the subtler meaning of metaphors and even poetry is often lost on me. There's something about a simple story that brings a message to life. Except, of course, for user guides and manuals; being a hands-on person, knowing how to do things can be very helpful, making those books relevant, therefore easy to read.

As might be imagined, the story of a God, an almighty Father who could chase his children—his own kids!—out of the Garden of Eden—their *home*—for having eaten an apple, or even worse, who could sacrifice His only son in a horrible, violent manner to save the rest of us from our sins, never really sat well with me. So I looked for a better story in other teachings. My preference was for stories about spiritual quests, usually as told in biographies or works of fiction rather than works containing complicated spirituality and theology, although I did read my fair share of those too. While I say "read," this does not mean that I understood everything I read, nor that I remember much of it. In fact, very little of what I read from hundreds of books remains in my memory banks. What I do recall is that I enjoyed inspiring stories, those that left me feeling as though I was more for having read the book.

Fast-forward to the present day, my preference for a good story has not changed, and so my recent distracting foray into the craft of fiction writing wasn't too much of a stretch. I was looking for a story that might reflect my shifting understanding of reality, one that would inspire me and take me to that feeling of being more. Being neither scientist nor theologian, I searched for new perspectives that would corroborate my expanding awareness of the meaning of life and the world in popular books, movies and television series. Curious about the future of humanity, I broadened my search to include stories in the science fiction genre. There must be others who were curious about another way of being in the world, one that would break the boundaries of traditional storytelling, or so I thought.

While researching storylines, I was taken aback by the growing number of end-of-world scenarios. For the most part, dystopian themes have replaced the utopia of old. Of greater concern is that many of these stories are geared toward youth. Most propose a future in which humanity must suffer some form of cataclysmic loss or at least be taken to the brink of annihilation before entertaining the possibility of an alternative scenario. Gone is the utopia of old. The ancient "heaven on earth" option has been completely overshadowed by a more "realistic" view, which really means a more dramatic and exciting view. The promise of an eventual Armageddon has taken root and is nurturing a culture of fear in humanity that feeds a need for increasing self-protection while fuelling divisiveness, hatred and distrust.

At first, I was troubled to learn from parents that their children enjoyed these stories, that they did not seem to find them disturbing. Upon closer examination, I came to see this as perhaps a good sign, a call from the still, small voice within. It has become clear that something *must* come to an end. In a way, those who find dystopian themes appealing may be closer to experiencing their sense of eternal self than seems apparent. The current state of humanity *is* dystopian. The more that technology advances, from growing food to building homes and the weapons needed to protect ourselves from potential threats to our existence, the more confident we are in our ability to survive an Armageddon. While we have become adept at being in charge of and managing our lives, humanity continues to display inhumanity to man and disregard for our planet. It does not matter that we can invent and build and manufacture all manner of fancy devices, as long as one child starves to death today, humanity has not tapped into its true potential—the ability to know and express love for all. As the Course makes clear, what is not love is hate and so, yes, this dystopian condition of humanity must come to an end, as it does not reflect our true nature.

The battle of good versus evil begins with our decision to function and seemingly exist as separate, independent entities, disconnected from our Source, and, as a consequence, disconnected from each other. Because it is not natural, we must struggle hard to maintain the illusion of independence. Anything that might point to a different way of being, especially to a rejoining with the Oneness of Life, would constitute a threat to the separation fantasy, hence the frightening portrayals of invasion by powerful human, earthly or otherworldly forces. Our popular stories show us how much we love drama, danger and threat. We thrive on the excitement of fighting to protect ourselves and our loved ones against illness, attacks by others, economic downturns or environmental catastrophes. We have turned the maintaining of the illusion of separation into an all-consuming activity, an exciting game of life. To explore the unknown—to wonder if there might be another way besides this limited experience—is threatening to the ego because it leaves it vulnerable to the truth. The true source of all fear resides in the ego's fear of being revealed for what it is—an imaginary sense of self.

If the Source of Life is eternal, infinite and good, there could never be an Armageddon because that which is eternal must be immune to harm of any kind. So where do our end-of-world stories originate? Clearly, they must not be inspired by a clear sense of the true, eternal nature of life; rather, they must stem from a vulnerable, finite perspective, which can only be born of an imaginary sense of self. If our essential nature is like its Source, constantly in the flow of harmonious unfolding, we cannot expect to hold the pause button on the Infinite Movement of Life indefinitely, at least we cannot do so without feeling some form of discomfort. It takes a great amount of energy and effort to maintain this amount of illusion and to make it appear so real that we remain convinced of its existence. Since the world as we are experiencing it constitutes a limitation on our experience of Reality as infinite beings and is not real, it cannot be maintained forever.

Contrary to popular myths, when the dream, or finite perspective, comes to an end and is replaced by Reality, it does not end as a consequence of suffering, sacrifice, violence, war, devastation or even Divine intervention; these are fantasies born out of an imagined view of the world. This is what the ego would like us to believe and with reason. The ego thrives on fear and excitement, and since its existence is founded on a lie, it can only exist in fear and constant vigilance against threats to its survival. Since the ego sense of self is not real, the only annihilation it faces is its own, so it is in the interest of its survival that we remain fearful of anything that might jeopardize its fragile existence. These are the ego's dreams, and they have nothing to do with Reality. When you wake up from a bad dream you are having at night, you don't wake up to a better version of the dream, you wake up in the safety of your bed to the realization that the dream was never real.

> The belief in hell is inescapable to those who identify with the ego. Their nightmares and their fears are all associated with it. The ego teaches that hell is in the FUTURE, for this is what all its teaching is directed to. Hell is its GOAL. (ACIM, Chap. 15, p. 348)

The world as we see it—a world without love—does, and must, come to an end. It follows that when this world ends, the ego concept also comes to an end, for this world is little more than the product of imagination gone wild. This is the true source of inspiration for the growing number of end-of-world scenarios. It is, in fact, a sign that, although mostly unconscious at the moment, the soul of humanity is stirring and reaching out for more. Feeling threatened, the ego sense of a sleeping humanity is lashing out frantically in a last ditch attempt to keep us from considering another way of being, a way that would naturally lead to its dissolution. What would happen if we searched for and found another way of being? We might then abandon the old familiar way. If choosing peace instead of drama and excitement provided a far more satisfactory experience of life, the battle would no longer have a place in our lives. Since the battle belongs to the ego's scenario, as we withdraw from the illusory battle, the ego sense of self fades from our experience.

Those who are waiting for a new age or a messiah to bring a better way of living for humanity will be disappointed. Since our world reflects our beliefs and we choose our beliefs, we have the experience we have chosen and continue to choose. We have the conditions, the climate and the humanity that we are presently accepting, fostering and nurturing. No alien power or force beyond our control will entice or force us to change. Any future climate will be the result of our current choices. We are the next Messiah; we are the Second Coming. It is our time to wake up to Reality.

The only way to experience something different is to make a different choice *now*. Since this world, as we are experiencing it, is of our own making, we are not the victims of a predestined era, a divine plan, almighty forces or hidden powers in the universe. We are entirely responsible for the state of our current civilization. We are making it up. We are choosing it. This means that we are deciding whether or not we want to experience a fantasy Armageddon by continuing to project the ego's fears into the dream, into the limited human condition. Although this may not be received as a welcome thought, it does mean that we have the power to change our experience and that power lies within us now. The only one that can receive this as unwelcome news is the ego sense of self because it needs something or someone to blame for its misery. To accept this as a possible alternative to our familiar beliefs is a step in the right direction, a step toward the awakening of humanity.

If the awakening of humanity is inevitable, it follows that the collapse of the ego—that deeply feared Armageddon—is also inevitable. From the ego's perspective, there is absolutely no benefit to awakening. The myth of the fall of man may be seen as a projection of the ego's fear of its inevitable demise. Since waking up means rejoining, and thus saying "no" to separation, the domain of the ego no longer serves a purpose. The ego—the false sense of self—faces its fall. While awakening means the dissolution of the ego and the abandonment of the limited, made-up perspective, it means the bringing forth of the Self and the ability to experience with full conscious awareness All that is being in Reality.

The Purpose of Fear

The primary driving force behind most of the ego's invitations is fear. In fact, the ego seeks out fear because it validates its very existence. Difficult to ignore, fear strengthens the sense of separation. Rather than offering the freedom and safety we seek, it locks us into a state of ongoing vulnerability. If I can be threatened, if I am in danger of being hurt or harmed in any way, I must exist. I exist as a separate, unique individual; I am vulnerable, and I must defend and protect myself and my own, no matter the cost. Fear is the lifeblood of the ego; it serves to keep brothers and sisters separate from each other and is the poison that keeps humanity from experiencing its full divine expression. Fear locks us into a prison of self-protection and defensiveness. Fear keeps out love. However, as *A Course in Miracles* tells us, that which is real cannot be threatened; that which is unreal does not exist. To live in fear then is an attack on one's Self. It is the denial of our wholeness and constitutes an act of self-hatred, which is then projected outward to our brothers and sisters. The limited human condition is thus maintained.

The decision to explore the possibility that waking up might be an option is ultimately the biggest threat to the existence of the ego sense of self. From this perspective, it is easy to understand the prevalence of end-of-world themes in books and movies, especially now, as the soul of humanity is beginning to reach for more, in other words, beginning to awaken. To protect its fragile existence, the ego must distract us by presenting increasingly dramatic and horrifying scenarios of the future of humanity. From the perspective of a separated humanity, doom and gloom are becoming a likely outcome, increasing fear and the need for self-protection. Don't even think of another way; look at what will happen if you do—the world will be destroyed. Prepare to fight for what is rightfully yours, the ego suggests. But the only fight is the ego's fight to remain a player in a made-up world where children are growing tired of their foolish games. It is time to grow up and leave the playroom, a realization that is being expressed by the rising number of individuals who are choosing to refuse to listen to the ego's invitations. There must be another way, they say, there must be.

What the ego does not want us to know is that fear is never justified because awakening cannot lead to the disappearance or non-existence of any person or thing. That which is real cannot disappear, and all that can be experienced exists in Reality. Life cannot be destroyed, and existence does not end with awakening. To be awake is to be truly invulnerable. To be awake is to experience reunification with all that is. To be awake is to flow with the infinite possibilities of what Life is being. It means being completely and utterly safe. It is like turning on the light after having lived in a darkened room for a long time and seeing everything as though for the very first time. To be asleep is to fumble around in the dark, trying to imagine what we might bump into, cautious and fearful of what could cause us harm. Once the lights have been turned on and our eyes have adjusted to the light, Reality becomes clear and visible, and the meaning of everything that is there to be experienced is revealed. As long as we remain in the dark, we cannot possibly know the true meaning of what we are experiencing.

While we remain mesmerized by this imaginary world of our making, Reality patiently waits for the moment we release the ego's artificial hold so that that which is infinite can once again be experienced. Since this hold has no true power and can falter at any moment, it is only natural that, while we cling to it, we experience fear. However, in the presence of Love, fear cannot exist. As we move toward a new perspective, we may also experience faltering trust. However, it is only that which is not real that cannot be trusted. By abandoning our old views and engaging in a leap of faith, we can experience our true eternal nature and open ourselves to a world of infinite possibilities, harmony, peace, brotherhood and true creative expression. Only then can love emerge. Although it appears as though we are caught up in a deep sleep from which we cannot seem to awaken, we have simply forgotten that we are born of eternal Life and that Love is the true substance of our being. As such, we are invulnerable, forever safe and, above all, as expressions of the Creator, we are, and have always been, loved.

> You have one test, as sure as God, by which to recognize if what you learned is true. If you are wholly free of fear of any kind, and if all those who meet, or even think of you, share in your perfect peace, then you can be sure that you have learned God's lesson, and not yours. (ACIM, Chap. 14, p. 343)

The Alternative

If you have been wondering if awakening is in the cards for you, or if it is even possible at all, welcome to the club. After facing what seemed like an endless parade of clever distractions, I was finally able to settle down and begin to work on this book. Let me tell you that it wasn't easy; resistance to looking at the truth head-on was very strong! The part of me that wanted to wake up was in a deadlock with the part of me that clearly did not. I needed to release my resistance to awakening and, instead, pay more attention to my desire for awakening. From the perspective of the ego sense of self, waking up holds no appeal.

What we are being invited to consider is that we, as Self, are part of and have never been separate from the One Mind, that we are, in fact *mind*. Waking up is the result of abandoning the false structures developed in the process of concocting a separate independent-thinking individual self. Furthermore, awakening is happening regardless of whether or not we are aware of it. Everyone is waking up from the dream of the human condition because being awake is our true state while being asleep is not. Full conscious awareness of what Life is unfolding is natural, while ignorance is not. Our awakening was set into motion the moment we decided to explore and experience something that is not our reality, not our birthright, a limited version of our true Selves. The tendency toward normal will always prevail, and so awakening is simply a matter of allowing rather than something that is achieved through effort and struggle. Full conscious awareness as Self will emerge. The ego sense of self will fade away, since it is not founded in Reality and has no true justification for being.

Waking up is an experience of abandoning our imaginary state of separation and rejoining with the One Mind. The current discomfort experienced by many people today is the result of an increasing awareness of the fact that we, the brotherhood or sisterhood of man, have put our faith in something that is not real, something that is not our true Self or our divine, inner Self. We have put our faith in a limited view of the world, as we perceive it in its three-dimensional form, something that once held the promise of joy and satisfaction, but which has only brought disappointment. True joy does not come from the outcome of events in the world; it comes from awakening to the full knowledge that we are divine expressions of the Source. Ultimately, the motivation for awakening will not be found in the world; it can only be found in the quiet centre within.

There are many systems, approaches, techniques, teachings and methods that address the development of conscious awareness. We choose the path that best suits our needs but that, above all, reflects our desire and readiness to awaken. One thing the seeker needs to be aware of is that, since originally embarked on with a strong ego sense of self, the journey Home itself can become a distraction and a delaying manoeuvre. We must remind ourselves that the goal is available to be experienced now. Regardless of whether or not we are actively engaged in such a process, we are always standing at the threshold of choice between the dream and Reality, illusion and Truth. We are always free to choose to experience the fullness of our Being, just as we are free to choose to continue to have a limited experience of life, to remain in the human condition. Since awakening is a return to normal, there is no need to work at it. All that is required is that we be ready to abandon wilful effort and thus allow our healing to unfold naturally. The more we step back, give up control, let go of the need to understand and simply allow our Divine nature to be expressed, the easier our awakening will be.

What lies beyond the dream? The experience of our infinite Being is what awaits us when we awaken, and the function of Being is conscious awareness. What lies beyond the dream is being what God wills for us to be, our true Self as expressed by the Infinite Life Source. It can be helpful to remember that what God wills is always good, whole and loving. There can be tremendous resistance to accepting that there is life beyond the dream because it requires the relinquishment of the false self to which we cling for dear life, what amounts to a substitute or dream life. Being awake means holding no barriers between the Self and everyone and everything else. By dropping these barriers, we are open to everyone and everything that is being along with us. Awakening constitutes the full conscious awareness of what God or the Source is being at any given moment in any given person, thing or situation, from the flower in the garden to a neighbour strolling down the street.

Awakening Is for Everyone

As we begin to consider the radical idea that we are freely choosing how we live in the world and that we could just as easily choose otherwise—a freedom that always has been available to us—certain questions, even objections come to mind. For example, when we look around and see our brothers and sisters playing their very convincing roles in their games, it is fair to wonder if there could be any other way of being. It all seems so real. As long as none of our brothers and sisters appear to experience awakening or as long as there are no examples of another way of being in the world, the dream remains the only alternative and continues to be chosen and reinforced.

Any teaching that suggests that we could experience eternal life, complete healing, reversal of aging and a life of perfect harmony with all of our brothers and sisters as well as with our planet will sound like fantasy, foolish utopia, the stuff of fairy tales. Only very special individuals like Jesus or the Buddha, rare beings with the gift of divine benediction, can have an experience that goes beyond the limited human condition. Enlightenment is for the very holy soul. It is for special "highly evolved" beings, our spiritual idols. The rest of us lowly mortals must suffer through thousands of lifetimes, be purged of our sins and be forgiven for our countless misdeeds before we can even begin to consider that there might be a place for us in Heaven. We certainly don't deserve, much less should we expect, special favours from God. That would be the epitome of arrogance! Besides, as we have seen, the life of a Buddha would be boring. This is what we have been taught; this is what we choose to believe, and we blindly support each other by maintaining and feeding these limiting beliefs.

I spent the better part of my life in search of truth, knowledge and understanding, working at improving, perfecting and preparing myself so I could one day be worthy of earning that exalted state of enlightenment. One could say that I wore the cloak of "spiritual seeker," a role I played with total commitment and dedication from within the great game of separation from Source. Most of the teachings I encountered required a lifetime, even lifetimes, of stringent practice, the study of complex metaphysical and spiritual truths and rigorous self-analysis and self-correction. I willingly, if not eagerly, pursued these paths because, for as far back as I can remember, all I had ever wanted was to wake up and be free of this confining human condition. Many of these teachings promised release from the world through eventual enlightenment. With no real interest in being in a world of increasing complexity and materiality, so never really fully engaged, I had been looking for a way out.

For years, I believed that awakening was something that needed to be worked at, something that would ultimately result in liberation from the material plane and would lead to the attainment of a lofty higher realm. My entire perspective on life and the world changed when I realized that God, the Source of Life, is being Life everywhere, in everything and everyone, including *me*, regardless of my seeming defects. Everything is like its Source, perfect, whole and unalterable, including *me*, including *you*. There is no getting away from our Divine Source, nor were we ever apart from It. What may have been the single biggest lesson of my journey was when I understood that the goal is not to wake up and *leave* but rather to wake up and *live*. The purpose of every minute of every day is to know—"ac-know-ledge"—what our Source is being here and now.

Face-to-face with the truth, what seemed now like a senseless lifelong quest came to a screeching halt.

Awakening is not the result of study, no matter how dedicated one is to the pursuit of knowledge. In fact, involvement in a course of study, as I was learning, can get in the way of the experience, especially when it is accompanied by deep intellectual understanding and, in particular, confidence in that understanding. Although the ardent spiritual seeker in me took this as a slap in the face, my reaction was quickly replaced by a profound feeling of reassurance and, most of all, relief. I was tired—actually, very tired—of studying and searching; it was time for a real experience of Truth. Finally, here was an encouraging, though boldly different, perspective. Awakening is inevitable because it is our natural condition, our divine birthright, and this is true for each and every person on the planet, even the seemingly least spiritual among us. If we decide to make a different choice, that which is natural will unfold with ease. All that is needed is that we give ourselves permission to wake up.

As shared in *The Movement of Being*, once I realized that the search for intellectual understanding, though helpful for undoing false beliefs, had gotten in the way of an experience of truth, I discovered that I was missing one crucial component: feeling. "You won't understand your way into the Kingdom of Heaven," Raj reminds us frequently. I would have to let go of my need to understand everything and *feel* my way Home. This was a tall order for a prolific generator of thoughts such as me. In the presence of God, I would necessarily feel the Love that is the Breath of all life. Awakening would feel like something because it places us in the flow of life, and the flow of life is expressed as Love because its Source *is* Love. I understood why I had been so moved by a passage from a collection of conversations with a humble, 17th-century Carmelite monk.

> [I]n the winter, seeing a tree stripped of its leaves, and considering that within a little time, the leaves would be renewed, and after that the flowers and fruit appear, he [Brother Lawrence] received a high view of the Providence and Power of God, which has never since been effaced from his soul. That

this view had perfectly set him loose from the world, and kindled in him such a love for God, that he could not tell whether it had increased in above forty years that he had lived since. (*The Practice of the Presence of God*)

The simplicity of the message had struck me to the core, and the first few times I read the passage, I was moved to tears. With the intellect out of the way, my soul began to stir, clearing the way for an experience of that Love we so long for—each and every one of us. The truth is simple. I had already learned *of* the truth but now I *knew* it. God is kind, fair and intelligent, and, most importantly, God is Love. In the months that followed, I began to abandon my deep-seated beliefs in my unworthiness and allowed myself to be loved by God. I wept many times as I began to allow God's Love to fill my being. I saw how He had always been there, how He had heard my cries for help, answered my prayers, walked with me as I stumbled along on my journey Home, but mostly, how He had patiently waited for me to accept His love, and accept it I did. Once again, I wept.

Not so long ago, I might have said that an experience such as that of Brother Lawrence was completely out of my reach because I was not a monk, or a holy person, much less a saint. But I have seen that even the most ordinary person can, and will, know the all-encompassing Love of the Father, for that is what it is to awaken. More importantly, because it is our birthright, awakening is inevitable. In our dream state, we have simply forgotten that we are loved. Because Love is the nature of our Source and, being infinite and unaffected by our imaginings, it has never been withheld from us. All that is needed is to be curious enough to wonder if there might be another way or if there might be more to be experienced than this limited human condition.

Unfolding Naturally

When working with clients, I sometimes describe the intelligence and appropriateness of simply allowing one's unfolding to occur in the same way that we would respect and allow the rose to unfold to its full blooming beauty. I haven't met anyone who would recommend purposefully pulling on the petals to make the flower bloom faster. Many people put a lot of effort into controlling the unfolding of their lives through the use of wilfulness and manipulation, unaware of the fact that unfolding occurs naturally, regardless of and, much of the time, despite our interference. Our function is simply to pay attention and embrace and enjoy the beauty and intelligence of the natural expression of the Life that resides in each and every person and thing we encounter.

In the summer, I took a day off from writing and joined my daughter for lunch at her downtown apartment. I had some tempeh burgers for her to taste-test, one of my latest culinary experiments, and she needed an update on her numerology and astrology cycles. With a pair of 19/1s among her core numbers and an 11/2 first pinnacle, Natalie had lived a very full, active life, first as a dancer and then as a Pilates instructor and fitness trainer. She is the poster child for the successful Gen Xer: focused, creative, dedicated, highly energetic, strong and independent. As much as the numerologist in me was curious to know how she was faring, given the new numerology and astrology cycles she had just begun, the mother in me knew better than to interfere. While we sat in her backyard, with the sun pushing its light and warmth between lush branches, her cat Bowie sleeping on my foot and the bees feasting on the blooms of the nearby bushes, I felt guided to use a slightly different approach for this reading. Before embarking on the task of interpreting the charts, I simply asked if she wouldn't mind sharing how she felt her life was going at this time.

She paused for a moment, only a brief, pensive 19/1 moment, then began to calmly describe how she had lost some of the drive that had propelled her most of her life. She felt as though her life was on hold; as though she needed to pause. Then she related a story of how one day, while she was shredding cabbage for a batch of sauerkraut, it occurred to her that the food processor did all the work; there was no need to apply force or work hard at it. The same thought occurred while she was making a skirt and passing the fabric through the sewing machine—no need for effort there either, since the machine does all the work.

She then extended the same realization to herself. She was coming to the understanding that her wholeness had always been there, simply waiting for her to allow it to unfold. There was no need to push herself or exert tremendous effort. I was impressed—very impressed—and, yes, of course, proud as a mother might be to hear how her daughter had arrived at this profound realization all on her own, without the need for years of stringent spiritual discipline. Awakening *is* natural; it simply unfolds when allowed. The beauty of this story is that Natalie's middle name is Rose, and now Natalie Rose is embracing her unfolding and what a truly beautiful awakening it is.

CHAPTER 4

The Game Changer

There is a time when childhood should be passed and gone forever. Seek not to retain the toys of children. Put them all away, for you have need of them no more. (ACIM, Chap. 29, p. 680)

Playing a Good Game

Since we have all but completely forgotten our true origins as expressions of the Infinite Life Source, it may take some motivation before we begin to consider an alternative as radical as waking up, especially when life isn't all that bad. For many people, success is measured by the amount of abundance, privilege and good fortune they have been able to acquire as a result of self-generated effort, perseverance and will. Common to most teachings and belief systems is a theme of incompleteness and lack, where the good life must be strived for and earned, often as a result of great personal sacrifice and struggle and sometimes at great cost to others. As long as the choice for independence from Source is maintained, this perception will be valued, as not only does it make separateness seem real, it provides a sense of purpose for the dream story. One must search far and wide to find a teaching that expresses the contrary—that we are part of an infinite Oneness and, by virtue of our divine birthright, no struggle is required for us to experience our perfection and our abundance. In fact, such a view might be perceived as naive, even completely unrealistic, by those who value the rewards of personal effort.

One day, I found myself on the listening end, actually more like the receiving end, of an impassioned discourse on the perils of illness and the inevitability of death. While I knew very well that this person had no interest in anything even remotely "spiritual," I decided to have a little fun by poking at the boundaries of his beliefs. I casually suggested that perhaps it was time to question our views on sickness and death and explore the infinite nature of life. He immediately replied that no one else had ever done so, as though this was a good enough reason to accept, without question, a cycle of birth, life, sickness and death.

The pursuit of awakening is not likely to appeal to those who are experiencing ease and worldly success, especially if they are confident in their understanding of how things work in the human condition. For those who identify strongly with and have no reason to question the ego-sense of self, the idea of being in a radically different way may even appear offensive to their intelligence. As long as there is the slightest chance that life might get better, that success might eventually be achieved, that something here in the limited human condition is worthy of our attention or that a sufficient level of comfort and ease can be sustained, in all likelihood, the idea of waking up will not hold any appeal. While awakening is available to everyone, it does not mean that everyone will be interested in exploring it at this time.

Whether or not we are successful in the eyes of the world, we all develop and maintain roles that ensure even the most basic level of survival in the human condition. These roles, the games we play, become essential aspects of our self-definitions; they form the foundation of our very existence. Take these away, as in the case of the loss of a job, or material loss through misfortune or illness, and we are likely to crumble in the face of the great unknown. The willingness to abandon confidence in the familiar way of life and place our trust in a new way of being requires a very real need for change. When the game of life is good, or even if it provides only a small benefit but holds the promise of more, there may not be sufficient incentive to pursue something as unusual as being awake.

We are not likely to seek out another way unless we find ourselves at the bottom of the barrel, or when the old familiar way has grown unbearable. Please, God, help me; I don't know what to do; I can't continue on my own. "I need help" are probably the least ego-friendly words. The moment things are under control and life returns to normal—the pain subsides, an illness is healed, an agreement has been reached, the problem is resolved, or the situation becomes manageable or at least relatively comfortable—we turn our attention back to the dream. Instantly, we are sucked into the first tolerable drama we encounter.

Each time we overcome a hurdle, each time we get back in the game, confidence in our ability to be in this world is reinforced. Since life is tolerable most of the time, and severe crises are relatively infrequent, at least the crises that move us to drop to our knees in prayer, awakening can seem to be a lengthy process, something to be looked into later in life, maybe. Even if a difficult situation has brought us a moment of profound insight or a sense of closeness to God, automatically, like a spring-loaded lever, even if we are genuinely grateful for God's help, our attention turns back to our story in the game we call our life. We don't need God when we are managing to play a good game in the dream.

While challenges and difficulties are often seen in a positive light because they can prompt us to rise above our limitations, the best-kept secret is that the overcoming of difficulties is not a requirement for waking up or for experiencing our wholeness and perfection. There is always only one cause of discomfort or lack of ease of any kind, and that is the decision to resist the expression of our true nature. To accept a limited experience as beings that are separate from the Source is unnatural. It is actually an act of aggression, an attack on our unlimited wholeness, hence the constant struggle that is experienced in the human condition. The effort we value in the daydream is a reflection of the effort required to maintain an unnatural condition. We are attempting to maintain an illusory condition of limitation and imperfection in the face of our true condition as divine, whole, perfect expressions of infinite Life.

If it is true that we are choosing our experience, it must mean that we actually value being separate from our Source—no matter the cost, no matter that our peace is compromised, no matter that our experience of life is significantly reduced in scope. We take pleasure in and derive satisfaction from the experience of autonomy, self-will and independence; without question, we accept and support the ego's definition of who we are. Even if we are experiencing a very minute portion of our Being, or are experiencing lack, difficulties, pain and suffering, the daydream is still preferable to an experience of Reality, the Kingdom of Heaven, that distant, unreachable place we hear about in our teachings. By opting for what is familiar and manageable, we are effectively sacrificing our wholeness for a shadow of our true, infinite existence, even if it means that death is the inevitable outcome. If we can manage to have a few good years, then the sacrifice seems worthwhile.

The Game Changer

Those who have hit the bottom of the barrel one time too many or those who just can't seem to play a good enough game are most likely to seek help, and may even be in search of a miracle. The term "miracle" as it is used in *A Course in Miracles* can be a bit baffling, at least at first glance. It doesn't sound like the miracles with which we are familiar, such as raising the dead, walking on water, healing the sick or turning water into wine. *Canadian Oxford Dictionary* defines the miracle as "an extraordinary event attributed to some supernatural agency." Most of us have understood miracles to be rare occurrences, extraordinary feats accomplished by exceptional individuals, if not by the hand of God Himself. From the very first pages of the book, it becomes clear that the meaning of the term "miracle" is truly unique. The miracle, the Course explains, is a correction. A correction is a measure employed when an error has occurred, and an error is nothing more than a mistake.

What is the mysterious mistake that spawned a 1300-page book called *A Course in Miracles*? It is our collective decision to believe that separation from our Source is possible. The miracle, as defined by the Course, is a shift in perception; it is a correction of the way we look at and see things. But what exactly does that mean? Why should we be concerned with "miracles" when we have some tangible situations to deal with in our everyday lives? The great strength of the miracle is that it will correct any mistake, big or small, according to the need, and everyone knows that humanity's need for correction is great. It is as gentle as a mother's love and powerful enough to remove whatever it is that keeps us from experiencing our wholeness. Yet, no matter their nature or seeming severity, all mistakes stem from the one incorrect belief: that it is possible to exist separately from our Source—to live apart from God. That is the only error that needs to be corrected.

> The miracle makes NO distinction among degrees of misperception. It is a device for perception-correction, effective quite apart from either the degree or the direction of the error. This is its TRUE indiscriminateness. (ACIM, Chap. 1, p. 17)

The miracle is a call for an adjustment to the way we see everything. It is like an update or rebooting of our system of perception. It is a tug from the still, small voice within that asks us if we might be willing to consider another way of being. It's time for an upgrade, it says quietly, and, sometimes, when we encounter resistance, not so quietly. It invites the children to stop playing their games a moment and wonder if there might be something else to do upstairs, or perhaps a great outdoors waiting to be explored. It is what has brought us to this point of being curious enough to take a close look at our beliefs. It is the tiny, sometimes annoying, voice that is requiring that we express more of who and what we truly are and that, above all, we recognize, honour and respect ourselves as expressions of the divine Source of Life.

The miracle fans the flames of curiosity about life, about creation and about who we are as sons and daughters of a loving God. It fuels our courage to question everything we know and presses us to uncover what lies beyond the limited human condition so that we may experience the full nature of our infinite Being. The miracle bridges the gap between the daydream, the illusory world of separation, and Reality, the ongoing movement of creation. It fosters our awakening by allowing us to safely and comfortably release the definitions we have accumulated while playing our imaginary games of separation.

The miracle is natural; in fact, the miracle is inevitable. It is inevitable because it brings us back to our true condition as whole, perfect expressions of the Infinite Life Source, as integral, essential, intelligent, creative aspects of the One Mind. It is the correction for the silly idea of separation, a mistaken belief that cannot be sustained in perfect Oneness. The miracle is as natural to our Being as breathing is to our limited experience of a self that seems to reside in a body. From the perspective of the ego, it is the ultimate game changer—the way out of the illusory game of separation. While the miracle may be the ego's greatest enemy, it is our strongest ally.

> Miracles occur naturally as expressions of love. The real miracle is the love that inspires them. In this sense, everything that comes from love is a miracle. Miracles are natural. When they do NOT occur something has gone wrong. (ACIM, Chap. 1, p. 2)

Why should we bother with, even expect to experience, the miracle? Don't you have to be some kind of special person for that to happen? I mean, I'm just an ordinary person. It is our birthright, our inheritance, as expressions of the loving Source of infinite Life to experience the miracle—each and every one of us. To experience anything less than the ongoing movement of Life that surrounds us is to settle for so little; it is to settle for crumbs from the table of Infinite Abundance. To accept the miracle is to set aside our childish games of pretend, to grow up and remember our true Self. It is to uncover, release and freely express our true purpose in life. To accept the miracle is to open the door to our awakening, relinquish our limited views and beliefs and recognize the meaning of everyone, everything and every expression of life in and around us. It is to let go of everything that is not true about us, all the lies we have invented, accepted, invited and nurtured—all the false definitions about ourselves. The miracle helps us embrace our wholeness, honour our integrity and allow what *is* to *be*, naturally, gracefully and without effort. With the help of the miracle, waking up becomes a simple matter of letting go, allowing what is natural to unfold and revelling in the harmony, beauty and intelligence of this unfolding.

> This is the only thing that you need do for vision, happiness, release from pain and the complete escape from sin, all to be given you. Say only this, but mean it with no reservations, for here the power of salvation lies:
>
> *"I AM responsible for what I see.*
> *I chose the feelings I experience, and I decided on the goal I would achieve.*
> *And everything that seems to happen to me*
> *I asked for, and received as I had asked."*
>
> Deceive yourself no longer that you are helpless in the face of what is done to you. Acknowledge but that you have been MISTAKEN, and all effects of your mistakes will disappear. (ACIM, Chap. 21, p. 502)

Not So Fast, Buddy!

Perhaps you have never pursued a spiritual path of any kind, or perhaps you have spent a lifetime chasing after that elusive goal of higher consciousness or awakening; either way, whether you are a beginner or a seasoned seeker, waking up is for everybody, and it is available to each one who desires it right now. There is no need for a long, suffering journey of self-perfection. Phew! That being said, if awakening is so simple, if it is our birthright and if it is available to us now, are we going to wake up now? Probably not. Why is that? If it's so simple, why can't we do it now? Why can't we just snap out of it and experience our wholeness, our perfection, our "divine birthright" now?

It's not so much that we can't, but rather that we are not likely to choose it, at least not right away. For a number of reasons, whether we are playing a good game or having the worst game of our life, we still prefer to cling to the error. While we are very familiar with the limited human condition, we have no idea of what the state of being awake will mean. We are being asked to give up our familiar sleeping state in favour of the unfamiliar state of full conscious awareness.

Maybe life has been difficult, and now you are facing the option of trusting that God, who is *being you*, will help you unfold into your full Being, if only you will give yourself permission. But, your ego-identified self chimes in, why would God spare one nanosecond for a worthless twerp like me? It is best to err on the side of caution and stick with the familiar, even if life is really shitty. I'd rather have a life in which I have some control than risk the chance that the life God has planned for me will suck. And so it is that, once again, our curiosity about experiencing what God is being in us slips from our awareness.

Awakening requires rejoining with the Oneness of which we are an integral part, something that is contrary to our current experience of independence. As long as we derive sufficient satisfaction and benefits from playing the game of separation, we will gladly delay awakening. Because the ego is entirely at the mercy of our attention, in order to protect its status, it will present us with an endless array of tantalizing longings and desires to ensure that we do not turn our attention elsewhere, especially not inward. From the perspective of the ego, turning inward is not an option because that is where the voice of our true Intelligence can be heard—the still, small voice within. Bring on the drama, the ego declares. As long as we are busy dealing with worldly problems, pursuing exciting goals, involved in challenging, stimulating activities and engaged in emotionally charged interactions with our brothers and sisters, we are not listening for the voice of sanity. The ego wins yet another battle for our attention and lives to play for another day.

> The distraction of the ego seems to interfere with your learning, but the ego HAS no power to distract you, unless you GIVE it the power. The ego's voice is a hallucination. You cannot expect it to say "I am not real." (ACIM, Chap. 8, p. 173)

Another favourite form of ego distraction with which we are all very familiar is thinking—uncontrolled, undisciplined, free flowing, independent thinking—a habit that is very difficult to break. While we are busy thinking, we cannot hear the call of the sane inner voice as it invites us to consider that maybe, just maybe, what we are experiencing is not the truth. In the presence of thinking, Knowing is inaccessible, and it is that Knowing that is the evidence of our true nature as expressions of the Infinite Mind. As long as we identify with the ego sense of self, we will maintain the amount of drama, busyness and mental chatter we can tolerate, just enough to keep us going, just enough to validate our distinct, unique existence, just enough to keep us from turning our attention within. While we continue to choose in favour of distractions, while we liberally exercise free will and make independent choices, we are oblivious to the nurturing, Infinite Movement of Life that is our Source.

One of the most challenging lessons of this new perspective is the realization that since we are expressions of the Infinite Life Source, we actually have no control over our lives. This means that we only have the illusion of control in a game of separation. Once we accept that God is our Source and that He is the cause of our existence—the Author of All that is—the ego ceases to be, for it loses its false sense of authority. This radical way of looking at life and the world may be difficult, or even impossible, to accept for those who believe that they actually have the power to make things happen in the world, for those who think they can control and influence the outcome of their lives with the use of free will and independent thinking. No one wants to play a game in which they have no power. What is not realized is that power exercised in a dream is illusory.

As we pursue this bold new perspective, the ego is likely to jump in and attempt to instill fear, doubt, even ridicule, but it is not in charge of, nor is it involved in, our awakening. Since the ego has no foundation in Reality, all it can do is send out suggestions, nothing more than empty, meaningless, powerless invitations. Because we always remain free to choose which voice we will listen to, the voice of sanity or the voice for insanity, the only power the ego has is the power of suggestion. Since its existence is false and it is subject to instant annihilation should we choose another way of being, it must find effective ways of attracting our attention, and it will do just that. It is like a magician using distractions to keep us from turning our attention to Reality; without our attention, it cannot survive. It will use any means possible, many of them very clever—actually, each one more clever than the last—to keep us from pursuing our path of awakening.

The ego would like us to believe that what lies beyond the limited three-dimensional world is a vast nothingness into which we will be swallowed up and made to disappear. Whether we call it Heaven, the higher realms, the afterlife or by any other name, from the perspective of the ego, waking up means death and the disappearance of all experience as an independent, separate self. It will do whatever it takes to frighten us so that we will not explore anything beyond what we currently accept as reality. To believe that the universe and, more importantly, *we* would disappear upon waking up is a surefire way of keeping us from pursuing it to completion.

One thing the ego will not share with us is that, whether a situation that grabs our attention appears positive or negative, good or bad, joyful or tragic, an ego invitation is just that—an invitation. Since the ego thrives on attention, the most powerful weapon for silencing it is to ignore it. The good news is that awakening does not require that we spend any time analyzing its invitations before rejecting them any more than we need to analyze a dream we had at night before tending to our daily activities. A simple *no*, and sometimes a very firm *no*, will suffice. In fact, to study and analyze the ego's requests is to give it a presence it does not have; it is essentially a waste of time. Since to be awake is our natural condition, we really can't mess it up; but since we are free to choose our experience, we can delay our awakening for as long as we choose.

The true Self and the ego-sense of self are easily distinguished by the differences in their style, content and motivation. The false self functions as though it were possible to be independent from the whole; it is often noisy and dramatic, self-reliant, autonomous and wilful and is always focused on its own interests. It will immediately balk at any attempts made to relinquish control, to abandon the use of independent wilfulness and to trust in something greater than itself. The true Self knows no fear, it trusts in the innate harmony of the flow of Life, it knows no bounds, and it meets our needs with intelligence and with love. While the true Self tends to our individual unfolding, it always fulfils the greater purpose for all of creation.

Giving Up the Game

To maintain our prized state of independence from Source, we must sacrifice the experience of Oneness with All that Is. This is indeed a very high price to pay for a state that is nothing more than an illusion, a childish game of pretend. This must mean that we believe that the cost of abandoning our limited condition is greater than the cost of maintaining it; otherwise, we would abandon it in an instant. What is it that we value so highly in the human condition that we are willing to sacrifice our full experience of Reality for it? What do we think will be the cost of giving up our illusions in exchange for an experience of full conscious Being?

We are now learning that the quickest way to attain the goal of enlightenment or to wake up to Reality is simply to allow what *is* to *be*. From the perspective of one who has not only adopted an ego sense of self but has also developed and nurtured it so well that there remains no recollection of there ever having been another Self, to *allow* does not make any sense. It certainly is likely to hold very little appeal. The ego defines its existence by its achievements and the results of its independent efforts and cleverness. To allow what *is* to *be* is contrary to the prevalent attitudes of focused effort, determination, accomplishment, self-determination, achievement, autonomy, free will and independence. We will ask a young person about their life goals, or an up-and-coming manager about their targeted quotas and achievements. Nobody ever says to simply be curious about what God is being in you, or allow what *is* to *be*. Such an approach would be perceived as passive, even weak and lacking in healthy ego ambition.

We define, evaluate and understand our experiences based on sensory data but also on history, memory and learning. *A Course in Miracles* challenges our confidence in what we think we know in the early Workbook Lessons, where we are told that nothing we see means anything, we do not understand anything we see and, to add insult to injury, our thoughts do not mean anything. To experience our true wholeness, we must be prepared to abandon the meanings we have attributed to the roles we play in the game of separation and trust that we are more than the self with which we are familiar.

We know ourselves by our accomplishments, by what we do and how we do it, by our name, culture, family and history and by our standing in the community. We know ourselves by a set of limited definitions that suit the ego's frame of reference rather than by who we are in Reality. I am a schoolteacher; I am an engineer; I am a CEO; I am a lost soul; I am a successful business person; I am a man; I am a woman; I am a parent; I am a writer; I am a spiritual seeker; I am an old soul; I am the victim of a chronic illness; I am socially awkward. There is a great fear of loss at the thought of abandoning these definitions of ourselves, no matter how limiting they may be.

The closer we get to the light, the harder we must work to generate and maintain darkness, for darkness cannot exist in the light. Just as darkness is not natural, neither are sin, illness, lack, suffering and death. In an enlightened world, the battle of good versus evil no longer exists because in perfect Oneness duality does not exist. One might ask, am I ready to give up the battle, the thrill of the challenge, or the satisfaction I derive from all that hard work? Or, am I ready to give up the more subtle satisfaction derived from my repeated failures, from my profound suffering? Inability to thrive in the daydream is just another excuse for turning down the invitation to explore wholeness and perfection. Who *me*? I could never be worthy of entering into Heaven!

Right now, we do not know how things will be when we awaken, or even if it is achievable. It is also true that we have no guarantees that we will derive any satisfaction or validation once we are awake, at least not from the perspective of the human condition. Besides, we have no proof that there is actually something beyond our current level of experience, at least something that is accessible to us who are still entrenched in—or perhaps more accurately, still enchanted by—the human condition. It takes courage to embrace this bold new journey into unknown territory, especially when we do not know if awakening will cause us to lose all that we cherish in the human condition. If life isn't that bad, we will be less motivated to take an unnecessary risk.

To add to our hesitation, we might wonder, if waking up is so simple, why does it seem so difficult to attain? Waking up only seems difficult because, in our intense immersion in the dream, we have forgotten that there is another state of mind, another way of being. We have energized the dream for so long that it may take some time before its momentum is diffused. Only then can we begin to experience greater conscious awareness. This dream, or this fantasy game, has become a deeply engrained habit, one that we do not even stop to question.

For as long as we can remember, we have believed that we are bodies, that we must struggle to survive in a world of ongoing challenges and difficulties, ultimately face death and, beyond that, quite possibly nothing. The sensory experience has become an addiction without which we believe we would be lost, or worse, cease to exist. In the physical form, we have very little experience of anything other than what we can validate through our senses. Without an alternate frame of reference to consider, it is difficult to conceive of anything different. To awaken to full conscious awareness requires that we release our current concepts of who we are as bodies and consider the possibility that we are not what we believe ourselves to be, but rather that we are truly *Mind*.

The full experience of awakening requires that there be no more desire for separation, no more inclination to develop and maintain an independent self, no more interest in manipulating the situations that confront us in the game of life for our own purposes. Waking up means the abandonment of all prior definitions, very likely all learning as well as any expectations for what will be in the future. It also means letting go of control—Thy will, Father/Mother, God, not mine, be done. To awaken is to accept that we don't really have a say in the matter of our own Being. We are not the author of our life, God is. This may very well be the most difficult step to take on the journey of awakening because it requires complete trust in a God of whom we have very little knowledge.

Giving the Word

So how *do* we free ourselves from this decision to experience a dream instead of Reality? By simply expressing the desire to wake up, by giving permission for what is natural to unfold and, above all, by expressing curiosity—the same curiosity that drew us into the game of separation in the first place. It sounds simple, and it is simple, except for the fact that as long as we identify with the ego sense of self, we will experience obstacles along the way and it will seem more complicated than it needs to be. What can be helpful is to remember that our natural state of full conscious awareness as expressions of the Infinite Life Source has always been available to us. Waking up is not about doing anything to wake up; waking up is about wanting to no longer be asleep. For most of us, this requires a leap of faith—a giant leap of faith—and the courage to trust in our divine birthright.

The ego will do its best to sidetrack us by suggesting that by living a good life—that is, by continuing to play the game—we will have a place in heaven after our death. However, since death is not real because life is eternal, and since Reality is all that exists, it is not necessary to experience death in order to experience our wholeness in Reality. Our true nature as Mind exists beyond the birth, life and death cycle. We have never ceased being whole, infinite expressions of the One Mind.

Essentially, we have the life circumstances that support the experience we desire. However, desire exists only in a context of separation from the Source. In a fully awakened state, we are free of desire, since lack and need do not exist in perfect wholeness. Ultimately, the only desire worthy of our attention is the desire to experience our perfection. The desire to wake up and reach beyond the limited human condition must come from something that is not of the ego since the human condition is an invention of the ego. This means that there must be another part of us that exists besides the ego sense of self. This is the true Self, the voice of our Soul that is either ignored in favour of the ego or embraced as the preferred alternative. It is a desire that originates from our innate sanity, the still, small voice within that whispers, maybe, just maybe there is another way. It reminds us that what is natural will unfold, as it should, harmoniously and, above all, with ease, if we simply let it unfold.

Miracle at Bat

When unimpeded by past definitions and future expectations, we are free to experience all of what is happening in the moment, and what is happening is always being something new. Allowing life to unfold can be frightening because it means that we will be experiencing the moment without any controls of our own. However, when we do let go, there are no limits to our experience of what is being expressed in the moment, for we are then joined with the infinite movement of what God is unfolding, an unfolding that can be witnessed in everyday situations and events.

The day after the loss of his teammate José Fernandez to a tragic boating accident, Dee Gordon of the Miami Marlins hit his first home run of the year. As he tearfully made his way around the bases, he had no idea that he would experience what has since been called a "transcendent MLB* moment." When asked by CNN reporter Anderson Cooper what he had been thinking when he stepped into the batter's box, he replied that his only intent had been to honour his friend. Although Dee Gordon admitted to not believing in God, after having hit the ball farther than ever before in his life, awkwardly, he said, "If y'all don't believe in God, you might as well start. For that to happen today, we had some help." (Wikipedia)

Many have brushed off the reference to God, which, from the traditional view of God is understandable—what does God have to do with a baseball game? However, from the perspective of a divine Source that is expressed as all that exists in creation, Dee Gordon's statement makes sense. He was, at the time of hitting that ball, in the best frame of mind to express his divine Self. He was not thinking. His only desire was to pay homage to the memory of his friend. He had no personal gain in mind, no plan, nor was he trying to hit a home run or trying to be a hero. He just wanted to honour his friend by playing ball. Although he described the experience as a sort of "blackout," his experience is a wonderful example of what happens when the "self" is set aside, and the "Self" is allowed to be expressed.

> We pause but for a moment more, to play our final happy game upon this earth. And then we go to take our rightful place where truth abides and games are meaningless. So is the story ended. (ACIM, Lesson 153)

*Major League Baseball

CHAPTER 5

A Helping Hand

Today I will make no decisions by myself.
(ACIM, Chap. 30, p. 683)

Correcting the Thought of Separation

Throughout all levels of society, across all age groups, great pride is derived from individual accomplishment, especially when self-motivated and achieved with autonomy. We are coached and encouraged to take charge of our lives, to become masters of our destinies and to create the future we desire. We have the power to create the world we want, or so we are told with great enthusiasm. However, to function as self-governing entities is to function in a manner that is contrary to our true nature as integral parts of an all-inclusive Life Source. Independent authority is contrary to perfect Oneness. To be independent from our Source is to be disconnected from that which sustains and nurtures life; it is to choose against Life; it is the denial of one's true, whole Self.

To continue in this manner cannot lead to full conscious awareness because separateness is what gives structure and validity to the dream world—the domain of the ego. The apparent experience of separation serves only the self-sustaining individuality, the ego sense of self. Being unnatural and, most of all, nothing more than imaginary, concepts, perceptions and beliefs that emerge from autonomous decisions must constantly be reinforced and energized through wilful choice, as is reflected in our ongoing struggle for survival. Over time, the effort required to maintain this misdirected energy leads to exhaustion and begins to lose its appeal. Eventually, we reach a point where we realize that what we are doing just isn't working, and we are ready to consider a different way of being. The extent of our readiness will determine how far we are willing to go to explore and uncover another way.

If separation, or the decision to function independently from the Source, is the problem, then it follows that joining will help to rectify the situation. To continue to function independently and go along our merry way toward our eventual awakening, perhaps in a hundred, or a thousand lifetimes, would be to continue in the same manner as before—slowly and with unnecessary discomfort. The more comfortable we are in the dream, the less we will be inclined to pursue other options; the more uncomfortable, the more likely are we to seek another way. As with all things, it is our choice that will determine where we will focus our attention: toward making a better dream or toward awakening.

We are not required to undertake this unusual journey of awakening on our own. In fact, the Course asks us to do something that is contrary—maybe even offensive—to our natures as self-reliant, highly capable individuals. It asks us to join and not make any decisions as separate, autonomous individuals. Raj repeatedly points out the importance of joining with an awakened brother or sister as an essential step for our awakening. He also assures us that we all have been assigned a guide, an awakened companion, at the moment of our birth.

This may not be an unusual concept for those who have sensed a helpful presence at critical moments in their lives. But for most of us, the thought of engaging in communication with a guide who appears to exist only in our mind may seem a bit odd, if not altogether improbable, something reserved for psychics and channellers, certainly not for regular, down-to-earth folks. Most of the people I have spoken with who are familiar with guidance have actually not consciously adopted the practice of joining, nor have they fully understood its value or appreciated its importance. Yet, the willingness to join and be accompanied may very well be the single most important factor in facilitating and speeding up awakening.

Joining with "my guide" is not something I would have undertaken on my own, and probably never would have, had I not been introduced to the Raj Material. Why would I check in with an imaginary guide when I have the ability to make decisions in an intelligent manner all on my own in a very real, tangible world? I had made it through the first fifty-plus years of my life without too many stumbles and falls, and with all that hands-on experience, I certainly knew a thing or two about life.

To abandon confidence in our ability to evaluate situations and make decisions on our own can be challenging because these skills are well honed and deeply ingrained. Independent thinking is a hard habit to break, and it might be the most difficult obstacle to awakening. It is insulting to our hard-earned ability to be successful in the world to be asked to relinquish the one practice that got us there in the first place—independent, self-motivated thinking.

For those souls who are brave enough to embark on this strange journey of awakening, having a travel partner might be helpful. Admittedly, since humanity is experiencing its very first flickers of awakening, there are not many fully enlightened brothers and sisters on earth at this time to accompany and support us in our healing. However, I have observed that, as we move toward this new way of being in the world, somehow we attract new friends, those who share the same curiosity about our true potential.

Still, we could use some help from someone who knows the way Home, someone who is awake. To reach out to guidance is important for our healing because it means that we no longer desire and value being in a state of isolation, independent and separate from our Source. To reach a point where we no longer wish to be separate, where we understand that we can no longer pursue this journey alone is the best way to shorten this senseless journey of awakening. To join is to do things differently; this is what we are seeking—a different way of being in the world.

Just as we cannot have a conversation with someone who is asleep and one who is asleep cannot communicate with someone who is awake, we cannot communicate with an awakened brother without actually extending out of the dream state. To communicate, or to commune, with someone who is awake actually puts us in Reality, that state of conscious awareness that we seek to experience. To reach out and join with an awakened one will facilitate awakening more than to read books and study about awakening.

> Leave ALL deception behind, and reach beyond all attempts of the ego to hold you back. I go before you because I AM beyond the ego. Reach, therefore, for my hand because you WANT to transcend the ego. (ACIM, Chap. 8, p. 184)

Connecting with Guidance

Connecting with guidance is a practice that does require a certain amount of dedication and persistence before it becomes second nature. However, it is not as difficult or as complicated as it might seem; there is certainly nothing magical or esoteric about it. It is no more unusual than talking to oneself, something most of us do automatically throughout the day, although this chatter is usually engaged with the ego sense of self. All that is needed is to remember that separation is unnatural, while to commune, or to join, is natural. One simply needs to be open to the possibility.

I have found that many people have experienced, at least once in their life, a moment in which they sensed a presence nearby, a helping hand, a sign from the universe, a gentle caress or a word seemingly out of thin air. This usually happens when guidance is most needed, when there is the least amount of resistance to receiving help; it is received without question, with a simple knowing that it is real and true and, above all, that it is an expression of love.

The following is a straightforward and effective four-step method for connecting with guidance as taught by Raj. In his workshops, Raj assures us that we are never alone. From the moment we decided to embark on our exciting little adventure of separation, we were accompanied by a guide. While it is the function of our guide to show us the way Home, in deference to our freedom of choice, our guide will not interfere with our decision to remain in the dream. Being fully awake, our guide always remains available and simply waits for our request for help. Being the presence of Love, our guide will never ignore a call for help. If we do not hear clearly, it is not for lack of response on the part of our guide; it is simply a result of inexperience on our part.

The easiest way to connect with guidance is to bypass the intellect and approach the matter with the curiosity of a child, free of doubt and preconceived ideas. Hold no expectations other than to connect, be heard and receive a response. Know that if you have asked for help, you have been heard, for that is the nature of love. Since love is the condition of Reality, it remains with us always; love has never been, nor will it ever be, withheld. To reach out and request help is a significant step toward reclaiming our sanity as expressions of the One Mind. It is by joining that the belief in separation is corrected and the mind is healed.

First, be still. Employ whatever means necessary to be quiet, to cease all meaningless mental activity and set aside all mundane concerns. The daily practice of meditation can be helpful for training the mind to be quiet and is an effective way for preparing to connect with guidance. Sit in a comfortable chair, in any position that allows for the absence of distractions; in a quiet room, perhaps with a "Do Not Disturb" sign on the door; in a hot bath; in the garden; or, if all else fails, in your car, in the quiet of your garage. Lying down in bed is not as effective as an upright position because of the greater likelihood of falling asleep. Although adopting a meditative state is helpful when first learning to connect with guidance, with experience you can, and should, practise joining with your guide at all times of the day, no matter the circumstance. As added incentive to the practice of daily meditation, Raj shares the following:

> Now there are two things I want to share with you about meditation. First of all, meditating and moving into your peace is not just a matter of moving from an agitated ego state into a peaceful ego state. It is truly a movement out of the ego state altogether, out of the surface reactive level of conscious awareness. And the peace is not a different emotional state. It is a direct experience of the very nature of your Being. The peace that you access as a result of meditation is

literally you coming into the conscious, tangible experience of your divine Being. And peace is simply the first stage of your capacity, as it were, to experience your Self directly. (Auckland, NZ, 1989)

Next, state clearly and simply your desire to be in communication with your guide. Do not repeat your request like a mantra or an affirmation; rather, express it as a clear statement of your sincere intention to establish this connection, and then let it go. Repetition implies a lack of trust in your ability to connect, as well as a lack of hearing ability on the part of your guide. Even if you doubt that you will be heard, proceed as sincerely as you can and know that you have been heard. Remind yourself that it is impossible for love to deny a call for help.

Then, be still and listen for a response until you sense a connection, or for as long as is comfortable. At first, answers may not come right away, especially if this is a new practice. Since your guide is awake, you can safely assume that he or she has heard your request. It is your hearing or your ability to communicate that is in need of a little brushing up. When the urge to quit arises, give it a few more minutes. This strengthens your resolve to establish a connection and obtain an answer. After that, if nothing comes to you, then simply go about your normal business. Know that an answer is forthcoming, perhaps at a more appropriate moment, in a manner that will be easiest for you to receive.

Finally, expect a response. Raj makes it clear that this is an important step: it establishes that your intent is sincere, it opens the door for receiving help and it begins to foster trust, an essential component to any deep and true relationship. To simply ask a question and not expect an answer would be like casting a fishing line with no expectation of catching anything. Also, to expect a response is a clear statement of your sense of worthiness: you deserve an answer for the simple reason that you, as a child of God, have asked for help. There are no prerequisites and no conditions to be met before guidance can be received. All that is needed is to ask, be quiet, listen and expect an answer.

Sometime after having connected, an answer may come in a form that is easy to recognize, such as a flash of insight, an inspired vision, unquestionable clarity, a strong knowing or a simple sense of what is right. It may also come later, perhaps even when least expected: in a dream, on a social media post, in the words of a song or even on a billboard along the side of the road. With practice, guidance takes the form of a conversation between two beings, you and your guide, with questions being asked and answers being given. You may find it helpful to have a pen and paper handy to write what comes to you from guidance.

I have adopted the practice of keeping a small digital recorder nearby at all times to catch those precious insights received from guidance, either during meditation, while out on my daily walks, at night when I go to bed or sometime during the night. One of the best times for hearing guidance is first thing in the morning, before becoming drawn into the day's activities, when the mind is free of clutter and more open to listening. When playing back these recordings, especially if several days or weeks have passed before listening to them, I have, on occasion, been surprised by the depth and appropriateness of the guidance received.

It is possible to engage in conversation with other awakened brothers and sisters besides your guide or even with the Father directly. Raj reminds us that he remains always available to commune with us; all that is needed is a call for help on our part. It is also possible simply to join with the Holy Spirit, what the Course refers to as our "right mind." Since all minds are joined, our right mind is in communion with all awakened brothers and sisters; it is essentially our bridge to Reality. What is important is to feel comfortable enough to share openly, without self-editing, even if you feel like cussing a blue streak. Love is whole and sees with true clarity, so you will never be judged or condemned, no matter how angry, grumpy or frustrated you feel, no matter how badly you think you have screwed up.

It does not matter if the source of the guidance is clear or not, whether it comes from your guide, the Holy Spirit, God or a song on the radio. To focus on the source is a distraction. True guidance will always reveal truth, and it will always be intelligent and appropriate for the moment. At first, you may wonder if you are just hearing your ego; however, rest assured that the ego would never advise you to do something that clarifies a situation and brings you closer to awakening because awakening means the end of the separate sense of self. The ego's function is to distract us and prevent us from turning our attention toward Reality. If a bit of guidance has brought us even a tiny step closer to Reality, rest assured that it was not the work of the ego.

It is easy to identify which voice you have heard, the voice of the ego, or that of your guide or even your Self. When the answer is true, there is no emotional involvement; there is peace; there may be joy, but there is no sense of self-gratification, pride, self-righteousness or any form of self-satisfaction. What is important is not to make a big deal of it. Everyone has heard guidance at least once in his or her life; everyone can hear guidance more frequently. One person is not more gifted than another is in this simple practice. The difference is that one may be more ready and willing, therefore more open, to listening to guidance than another may be. That is the only difference.

But, I Can Do It Myself

Generally, we tend to ask for help when we are in serious trouble or when we can go no further on our own. In the face of a major crisis, a serious illness, for example, we may turn to God, or a favourite saint, and ask for help and pray for a miracle. As the crisis passes, healing begins, things calm down and we regain control of the circumstances of our dream life, we forget about that humiliating moment when we had no other choice but to reach out and ask for help. With renewed strength and confidence, we dust ourselves off, get back in the game and praise ourselves for a lesson well learned.

However, while guidance may have been present in the resolution of the situation, we mostly recall having overcome a difficult challenge with the use of our skill and wit, and maybe a bit of luck. We did it! We made it! Where a crisis might have led to increased awareness of our oneness with the Whole—our essential invulnerability—it remains little more than another event that led to greater confidence in our ability to be successful in the dream. We soon forget that ego-humiliating moment when we cried out for help; our dream experience is thus reinforced.

Although this may seem silly, or even a waste of time, in the beginning, it may be good practice to join with your guide and ask about simple, unimportant matters, those activities with which you are most comfortable and confident. Should I go to Costco today? Should I go for my walk now, or after lunch? Should I take a yoga break now? Should I make a new batch of granola today? I have found on numerous occasions that, had I not checked in with guidance, I might have gone for that walk and I would have missed an important call, or I might have been caught in the rain. When I check in with guidance, I am more likely to be where I need to be when it is most appropriate and beneficial. I have also learned that it does not matter if I think I have heard correctly or not. What remains important, always, is to join; if I think I heard incorrectly, so what. I checked in and that's all that matters.

Our entire existence in the dream is a mistake, so it's okay to hear incorrectly. What truly matters is that an attempt at connecting is being made because joining is the correction for the mistake of separation. In time, every minute of the day is engaged in partnership with our guide, with the Father or with the Holy Spirit. If an answer is unclear, ask again, but don't obsess or ask over and over again. Rest assured that if you have asked for help, your guide has heard you. It may be that you do not want to hear a response that may differ from the one that suits the ego sense of self. Ask yourself whether you truly wanted input, or whether you were seeking validation of a decision you had already made. It is helpful to pause a moment after asking a question; this way, the ego has less opportunity to jump in.

When I was searching for solutions for making tempeh, a fermented bean staple in Indonesian cuisine, I came upon a really neat new kitchen machine. *Yeah, buy that hot, new expensive tempeh maker!* my devilish independent voice said. *You deserve it.* This time, I paid attention to the quiet voice within, and I was advised to hold off on that purchase. Which is exactly what I did, and not long after, I found a solution for my tempeh-making problem, saving myself not only a bundle of cash but also prime storage space in my tiny condo.

When facing a situation, if we "think things through" and come to a conclusion or decide on a course of action before checking in with our guide, it may be more difficult to hear and accept guidance that is contrary to our independent conclusion. Generally, when we feel confident about our plan of action, we will be less inclined to check in with guidance. We go right ahead and hope for the best, maybe checking in along the way, but just to get approval for the choice we have already made. It is only when things don't work out as planned that we realize that perhaps we should have paid more attention to our guide.

Although I had been checking in with guidance when I went on my shopping sprees for the flooring and the frying pans and all the other silly distractions that kept me from working on this book, I was making the decision first. I need a new kitchen floor, I decided, after which, I checked in with my Friend. How about this colour? That was the wrong way of connecting with guidance. The point is to check in first. Had I checked in first and asked whether I should get a new kitchen floor, I likely would have gotten a "no" answer. In fact, I would have gotten a lot of "no's" that year. The purpose of the distractions during that period was obviously to keep me from working on this book, for writing had become a way for me to connect with God and with my Friend, and so this was not an activity that would be supported by the ego sense of self.

In the absence of a vested interest in an outcome or in the absence of a predetermined plan of action, it is easier to listen to guidance and accept a response. I find that if I am not clinging to a personal desire, I will not feel thwarted in my actions when my Friend responds with a "no" to one of my crazy ideas. There is no loss in abandoning independent decision-making, only a gain since joining takes us one step closer toward awakening.

Being from the independent or "unjoined" perspective likely indicates ego involvement. Even if in search of a positive resolution to a situation, when functioning independently, there usually is a subjective purpose, such as wanting to be right, wanting to be the first to find a solution, gaining approval, attention, power or a pat on the back. From that perspective, the solution may or may not be the best one. In fact, very often it is not the best solution because it is missing the broader perspective. All actions, decisions and thoughts that are performed without joining have the effect of reinforcing the illusion of separation, the illusion of being able to do things independently from the whole. It is the thoughts and actions that are inspired from within that are the most likely to contribute to the healing of humanity.

Another point about turning within, at least from the perspective of the ego, is that it is not rewarding. Checking in with guidance before taking action takes the fun and excitement out of trying to figure out what to do about a situation. No self-adulating ego wants to defer to a higher authority. No healthy ego wants to yield to a power or a decision-maker other than itself, for in so doing, it runs the risk of not being able to take credit for the outcome. I can do it myself, says the ego; I want to do it myself. Independent action and wilfulness validate the ego's existence. However, what the ego will not share is that one who is not joined with the Source is like a light bulb that is not in its socket. It cannot produce light.

Chaos, doubt and ambiguity create a climate of confusion, the happy place for the ego sense of self. Having gained a profound appreciation for simplicity over the last few years, I have adopted the following policy: when in doubt, do without. More often than not, I have found this to work quite well, saving time and energy from being wasted on senseless activities. All that matters is that I have stood down from the invitation to become lost in confusion, I have joined, asked for help and I have listened for an answer. After all, what we do in the dream, while in a state of limited conscious awareness, is of little consequence; it is how we do it that matters—whether we are joined or functioning as independent entities. It is the conscious desire to join that will bridge the gap between the isolation of the dream and an experience of Reality.

Ultimately, joining with guidance should be a normal, ongoing practice, whether dealing with simple, mundane events or facing difficult situations. In time, it becomes easy, even natural, to ask for help and to listen, and also to distinguish between the voice of the ego and the voice of guidance. As long as we continue to function as independent egos, the way Home remains obscured. When we have sufficient humility to admit that we would prefer to join than function independently, the way Home becomes clear. One other benefit of establishing a relationship with guidance is that it is likely to replace any feelings of isolation or loneliness with a feeling of safety and a sense of belonging. The greatest benefit of all is that, given that joining is an act of love, it feels so good.

As I approached the final draft of this book, I asked for help with the title. The original working title After the Miracle was okay, but I felt there might be a better one. I had already been told that the title would be made clear once the book was nearly done, and so I asked, once again, for help. "You already have it," my Friend told me; but I still didn't see it. The day after the first draft was completed I woke up with the title clear in my mind: The Healing of Humanity. Hmmm, I thought to myself, it's bold, but it makes sense, and so I took note of it. The following day, while updating the ISBN information for the book, I noticed a list of possible titles in the book data file, a file I had not looked at in over a year. The first title on the list was The Healing of Humanity. Okay. I had heard correctly, though still surprised whenever confirmation was encountered.

CHAPTER 6

Two by Two

The ark of peace is entered two by two.
(ACIM, Chap. 20, p. 487)

The Healing Power of Relationships

Allowing for varying degrees of sociability and preference for isolation, humans are essentially social beings. Since the human condition is nothing more than an experiment in separation from Source and has no foundation in Reality, for it to be sustained, there must be agreement and collaboration among its participants. However, because there is agreement and collaboration among its participants, it does not make the human experiment real. Since all-inclusiveness, or Oneness, is the true nature of Reality, no matter how real it may appear, separation remains a fantasy in the minds of the children who have decided to make up their own rules and engage awhile in imaginary games. It is this very collaboration that must be addressed if awakening is to be experienced.

Although what we do in the separated state is imaginary and can have no impact on Reality, it only takes a quick look around to realize that the game has become an intolerable distraction for far too many of its players. Having grown tired of their games, the children are looking for something more appropriate, perhaps more grown up, to which they can turn their attention. It is becoming increasingly difficult to ignore the fact that change is needed, that the human condition is deeply flawed and something needs to be done. Because each one of us is a divine expression of the Source, or God, each one of us is entitled to complete healing, peace and fulfillment, regardless of the role we have played in the separation experiment. Everyone deserves to experience his or her divinity, and for this to happen, we will need to choose to interact with each other in a different way, with a radically different understanding of the nature of our Being.

Wanting to be agents for change, many brave and caring souls are rolling up their sleeves and stepping in. Although efforts made from within the dream may bring temporary alleviation of pain and suffering, ultimately they will not bring the complete healing that is needed. If any efforts are to result in a valid and lasting contribution to the healing of humanity, we must step beyond the limited human condition to the realm of Reality. Since agreement and collaboration are at the heart of the separation experiment, for real change to take effect, we will need to engage with each other in a new way. The deeply entrenched, familiar ways of being in the fantasy world will not bring change; the old agreements that keep us bound to the game must be abandoned and replaced with new agreements.

A Course in Miracles places great importance on relationships, stating that, in fact, the healing of our relationships is at the heart of waking up. Awakening is not something that is accomplished alone or in isolation; it is the result of an act of joining because joining is what heals the belief in separation. Since awakening leads to an awareness of the Oneness of all that is in Reality, to maintain isolation or separation of any kind is contrary to the nature of Reality. If awakening is an experience of re-joining with all of creation, then the practice of any form of separateness, isolation or segregation for the sake of sustaining a private, self-sufficient, independent existence serves to reinforce the game of separation and is likely to delay awakening. Joining through the removal of boundaries facilitates the experience of awakening as it fosters the development of trust in something greater than the current limited perspective could ever provide. With practice, joining leads to the full conscious awareness of our Oneness with all that is.

Although from the perspective of the material world we appear to join as bodies, joining is actually an experience that occurs on the level of mind. Since all expressions of life originate in Mind, we do not have any experiences that did not originate as thought. Joining occurs on the inside, not on the outside; only minds can join, bodies cannot join. Furthermore, since everyone and everything is an integral part of the One Mind, whether we are aware of it or not, all minds are joined. This means that our thoughts are important for they contribute either to healing or to the maintaining of illusions. The only way to experience real change is to go to the source, the original thought that gave rise to the decision for separation, a decision we collectively made to have an experience of being in a way that is not our true way of being. As individual minds are healed, the mind of humanity also begins to experience healing, and in this way, all of our brothers and sisters begin to experience their own healing.

In the human condition, feelings of loneliness and isolation are almost inevitable. The discomfort of isolation is most commonly addressed by joining with others in the dream. Although somewhat helpful, this joining can never be fully satisfactory since it is the joining of two who are engaged in a game of separation, a condition that is contrary to the whole and all-inclusive nature of Being. It is a substitute for the true joining that is necessary for an experience of full conscious awareness. While these relationships, which the Course refers to as "special relationships," can keep us moderately satisfied while in the dream state, since they are founded on artificial roles and false beliefs, over time they are likely to lead to dissatisfaction. One has only to consider the growing number of failed relationships to see that the way we join with each other is in need of correction. Given that special relationships are a substitute for the true joining that is really needed, it is understandable why so many relationships fail.

While joining is essential for healing to be experienced, a distinction needs to be made between joining that is unhealthy because it sustains separation as is experienced in the special relationship, and joining that is healthy and promotes awakening, what is referred to in the Course as the "holy relationship." The two serve opposite purposes and can never be made to function in harmony. The special relationship is built on bargains and agreements and serves to validate the belief in separation, whereas the holy relationship is built on the acceptance of the Oneness of all that is. Until one answers the call for awakening and is ready to look with different eyes, it can be assumed that most, if not all relationships, whether family, personal, romantic, work or casual, fall under the category of special relationships. Once attention is turned toward another way of being and a greater awareness is sought and embraced, the special relationship can then be transformed into a holy relationship.

The holy relationship serves to release the mind from the thought of separation and facilitate its return to its original natural condition as an integral part of the One Mind. It can be helpful to think of the word "holy" as referring to wholeness or meaning "wholly" rather than the common religious sense of special, blessed or chosen. The holy or "wholizing" relationship is automatically engaged in when we join with one who is awake. It is only while engaged in a holy relationship that true joining occurs, and only true joining can lead to an experience of Reality. Joining in a holy relationship makes awakening more accessible and practicable while providing much needed companionship in what may seem like a strange or unusual pursuit. For the time being, at least until more of our brothers and sisters begin to engage in greater conscious awareness and can be from their right minds, a relationship with our guide or an awakened brother or sister is likely to offer the best support for our return to wholeness.

> The holy relationship, a major step toward the perception of the real world, is learned. It is the old, unholy relationship, transformed and seen anew. The holy relationship is a phenomenal teaching accomplishment. (ACIM, Chap. 17, p. 412)

The path to awakening is made easier when we consider that there are always only two choices. We can continue to choose to go through life independently, supported by others with whom we engage in special relationships, reinforcing the imaginary game of separation with and for each other. Alternatively, we can join in a holy or "wholizing" relationship with our guide, or an awakened brother or sister, someone who is truly capable of helping us wake up, one who sees the game of pretend for what it is and who can help us laugh it off and choose instead to become who and what we truly are. In the end, we determine our life experience by the relationships we choose to maintain—special relationships or holy relationships.

So it is that, at least until we have made a different choice, we are likely to seek out and attract individuals who, like ourselves, continue to choose to play the game of separation. When it comes to its own survival, the ego can be rather clever, which is why special relationships are so plentiful and come in a wide variety of shapes and sizes. At the top of its list of great accomplishments is the family relationship, the dynamics of which can be particularly revealing when attempting to identify whether we have chosen for the dream or for awakening, for illusion or for truth. Given their importance and high level of complexity, family relationships are valuable for the healing of all concerned.

From the day we appear to be born, that is, contained in a body, no longer experiencing ourselves as mind, our experiment in separation places us in the uncomfortable position of having to depend on others, whether parents or guardians, for our very survival. We learn that we are vulnerable, that we are finite, that we have needs that must be met or else we will be uncomfortable or worse, cease to exist. We are indebted to our caregivers, no matter the nature of the relationship. The seeds of powerlessness, dependency, weakness, guilt, resentment and obligation have been sown. With varying degrees of success, we then learn to obtain what we need for our continued survival by complying with, cajoling, managing, manipulating or controlling our environments. Nowhere are we taught that need, lack, and the struggle for survival all come from the separation scenario. We have forgotten that they do not exist in Reality, where there cannot be a lack of any kind.

In the family environment, beliefs, behaviours, ways of interacting with the world and with others are learned and repeated and become habits. While we are enjoying an experience of separateness, we may not be aware of this learning until we leave home and sometimes not until much later. Similarities in character, talents, skills, values, goals, needs and desires among family members may reinforce the family bonds, generating a sense of unity that can sometimes reinforce separation from others, those who do not belong to the family group. Family first, we say. Although it can provide a sense of safety, since it is exclusive and sustains the thought of separation this bond represents an incomplete sense of unity; it does not automatically ensure expressions of true all-inclusive love.

Sometimes, differences in character, interests, values, beliefs and goals may drive family members apart and lead to a search outside the family boundaries for like-minded friends. This kind of separation adds to feelings of guilt because society teaches us that the family bond is important. Yet, guilt exists only in the imagined scenario of separation from Source; it has no foundation in Reality. Independence is now reinforced by separation from the family group. There is the family, and there are my special friends, the ones who will validate my beliefs about myself. I exist apart from my family because we are too different from each other; we have nothing in common; separation is possible, and it exists. No matter the justification for separation, it is always an expression of the ego's desire to sustain the human condition.

> The search for the special relationship is the sign that you equate yourself with the ego, and not with God. For the special relationship has value ONLY to the ego. To the ego UNLESS a relationship has special value it has NO meaning, and it perceives ALL love as special. (ACIM, Chap. 16, p. 393)

Special relationships are not intended to facilitate healing and wholeness. We attract friends, co-workers, neighbours, adversaries, rivals and opponents who will support what we have chosen to believe about ourselves and about the world. As long as everyone agrees on the parameters, whether for good or ill, war or peace, conflict or harmony, danger or safety, the arrangement seems to work. Whether or not they started out on a positive, hopeful note, special relationships have the added advantage of providing us with convenient "others" who can be blamed for our troubles and suffering, or thanked for our opportunities and good fortune. When our special friends no longer support our changing views, we move on to other friends, those who will support our new perception. If the new friends establish a sense of distance or separation from the old friends, they are little more than a new group of special relationships.

To seek out a relationship to fill the loneliness and emptiness of separation always carries the risk of becoming a transactional relationship. Whether conscious of it or not, as long as both parties continue to choose separation, both will agree to support each other's roles. Because these relationships serve to maintain the illusion of separation, they do not constitute true, healthy joining and often end up becoming dysfunctional. This is especially so when, for whatever reason, one of the parties involved begins to reconsider the original agreement. As agreements are no longer sustained, the bonds of the relationship falter and sometimes generate conflict. However, by paying attention to the dynamics of these special relationships, it is possible to uncover the stories that keep us bound to the game. With growing clarity, it is then possible to experience release from the limited human condition.

Although far from perfect and still in the realm of special relationships, the love of personal relationships is the closest we have to an experience of the Love of God, and because they can contribute to our healing, they should be cherished and nurtured. Be it the love for a spouse, a child, a pet or even a plant, free of fear and uniting in nature, these expressions of love can help bridge the gap of separation. It is in these close personal relationships that we have the greatest opportunity to safely and gently uncover and release our beliefs about ourselves, those lies whispered to us by the false self, the ego. As we engage in a shift in perception, as we allow miracles into our life, our relationships flourish and healing is experienced.

> Heaven is the home of perfect purity, and God created it for YOU. Look on your holy brother, sinless as yourself, and let him lead you there. (ACIM, Chap. 22, p. 528)

Seeing Without Filters

The profound importance of what the Course refers to as seeing your brother or your sister "sinless," or seeing "the Christ" or the divinity in a brother or sister, may not be self-evident. For this reason, it is probably among the most overlooked steps in the healing of the separated mind. In the language of the Course, our brothers and sisters are actually our "saviours," our greatest teachers because they help us uncover how we see. Since there are only two ways of seeing, very little effort is required, and so insights are immediately available. In fact, all that is needed is a little willingness to see what is truly before us. If we are to experience healing as well as contribute to the healing of humanity, we will need to expand our vision beyond what we think we know, beyond the filters of our beliefs to see what the Source of Life is truly expressing in our brothers and sisters. Ultimately, we must be willing to look into our brother's eyes and remember God.

The Course defines "sin" as a simple error of perception or a mistaken way of seeing. Sin is born of the belief that separation from Source is possible and that life as a body, in a material world, disconnected from the One Mind is possible. To sin is to accept a limited life experience, lack, sickness, suffering, guilt, death and anything less than perfect wholeness. To sin is to choose what is not natural; it is to reject our birthright. How we see a brother or sister is significant because it reveals which experience we have chosen: fantasy or Reality. It reveals the lens through which we have chosen to see: the tainted lens of the ego or the clear lens of our right mind. To see a brother or sister in any way but whole is to accept a false scenario. By seeing sin instead of truth, by accepting the ego's lies instead of asking to see what is truly there, we cannot contribute to the healing of anyone; healing can only occur when we look beyond sin to what is true. To only see sin is to withhold the healing power of love.

Whether the connection is brand new, a passing encounter or a lifelong relationship, the setup is the same, and it is automatic. The moment we see the "other" as a body with a collection of attributes such as gender, age, race, culture or economic status, a judgment has been made. The mechanics of separation have been set into motion, and a special relationship has been chosen over a holy relationship. Even if we have never met the other person, perhaps we have heard of them through a friend or read about them on the Internet, the moment a judgment has been made the relationship's potential holiness has been set on the back burner. The ego sees only form; being bound by judgment, it cannot grasp true meaning. If we have not seen the light, the energy, the wholeness and the beauty of the divine expression that is before us, if we have not felt the love that is the reason for their Being, we have not experienced them as they truly are. Being an expression of separation, the ego cannot experience what is available only to the healed—whole—mind.

Why do we continue to experience limited perception over full conscious awareness? Chances are that we have not yet gotten into the new habit of asking, Father, what is my brother expressing as your son? What is my sister being as an expression of your Love? We fall into the old, habitual way of seeing with the eyes of judgment, through the filters of past experience, learning and beliefs. Out of habit, we forget to do the one thing that will bring us into that greater awareness where truth is available: we forget to join with our guide. Again, out of habit, we forget to take a moment to remember that everyone and everything is an integral part of the one, whole, perfect Mind. Until we desire to experience full conscious awareness above all else, we will continue to look through the tainted lens of the ego. From this limited perspective, we will continue to cheat ourselves of the opportunity to share in the awesomeness of the Movement of Creation.

Perhaps we have not yet developed these new habits because we have not realized that encounters with our brothers and sisters are the keys to awakening. When we choose to look with the eyes of judgment or when we focus our attention on the roles being played, it is ourselves we are hurting. By refusing to see the truth in another, we are likely coming from fear, and where there is fear, love cannot be. We then severely compromise our experience by withholding the one thing we need most in our lives—love. To withhold love is an attack on our wholeness, a rejection of our integrity. To be the presence of love, we must abandon the fear that causes division, for love can only be expressed in the absence of fear. Only in this way can we give to the world what is most needed at this time. If we truly want a different experience, we will need to consistently apply a new practice.

To see someone as an expression of God, especially someone with whom we have a history, requires letting go of definitions, judgments, beliefs and, probably the most difficult to release, memories. We cannot truly love our brothers and sisters as we perceive them or define them from within the limited framework of the game of separation. This false perception covers up its players with costumes that have been assigned within the game by those who have agreed to limit their experience to the human condition. These costumes and special roles must be abandoned before true love for another, as well as for ourselves, can be expressed. The great news is that, since these perceptions are based on experiences that are without foundation in Reality, they do not need to be ferreted out and analyzed, and can easily be released. It takes only an instant to say yes to love and no to fear. Free of the limitation of faulty vision, the way is made clear for an experience of the truth.

> Vision will come to you at first in glimpses, but they will be enough to show you what is given you who see your brother sinless. Truth is restored to you through your desire, as it was lost to you through your desire for something else. Open the holy place which you closed off by valuing the "something else", and what was never lost will quietly return. (ACIM, Chap. 20, p. 495)

It is only when my Friend pointed out that because I have not seen beyond the roles and the games being played or, because I have not seen wholeness—or holiness—in my brother, it does not mean that my brother is defective. No one is defective in truth or in Reality. It only means that *my vision* is temporarily defective. That little tidbit of insight made me sit up and pay attention real quick. I didn't like that my vision was defective. However, correcting vision may not always be as easy as it sounds. There are times when it is difficult to see the holiness behind the prevailing "assholiness" of a brother. The automatic response is to point out the unholy behaviour or sometimes to attempt to make the other change the behaviour. But, if real change is to be experienced, a new way of seeing must be embraced, and since a new way is what we desire, then we shall persist and try, once again, for that miraculous shift in perception that will allow us to know truth from direct experience.

Why should we focus on coming from love and seeing the innocence in our brother? How is seeing a brother sinless relevant and why is it important for our own awakening? My Friend shared the following insights on these, and similar questions.

"When you are seeing a brother who appears to be behaving in a way that is not enlightened or not whole, it does not mean that his wholeness or his enlightened Self is not available. It is there now, it is not something that is going to be there one day when he attains enlightenment. It is up to you to see that *now*; it is already available for you to see, it has not been destroyed or taken away nor does it need to be developed or earned. Because a brother chooses to misrepresent himself, in other words, misrepresent the child of God that he truly is, it does not mean that you must agree with him. Your job is to see the Christ no matter what the behaviour is. You are to look into your brother's eyes and remember God.

"Know also that it's never about your brother. It's always about *you*. When you come from a place of peace and love, you are heading toward your own awakening; you are in your right mind, expressing your own divinity. Do not be concerned about the other's response. You do not bring another person to the light. You become the light for the other person to see, and then they can choose whether or not they want to shift toward more light for themselves. You don't give love to another, or bring another person to love, you *be* the presence of love yourself. Again, the other will decide whether they want to experience this love now, or whether they want, for a little while longer, to cling to the absence of love.

"A different point of view, a different way of looking or a different way of seeing is not a different opinion about the world or the dream. It is a different vantage point from which to look at the situation, a perspective that provides a completely different picture of what is going on. From this new point of view, you can see, for example, that someone who appears to be expressing anger or hatred is actually calling for love. They are coming from a place of self-condemnation, even self-hatred. They are reaching out and asking the world to prove either their unworthiness or to give them what they are truly seeking, what they truly need—love.

"What God is being in the other is always dominant over what the other is expressing as an ego, no matter how dramatic may be the ego expression. What God is being in the other is the only thing that is real. What the ego is expressing is not real and has no power unless you believe it can have power over you, and unless you give it power. It only seems to have power over a made-up, vulnerable, fantasy you, one that is not what God is being. Remember that what God is being is always loving, intelligent, safe, invulnerable, infinite and eternal, and *God is always being you, and God is always being your brothers and sisters.*

"When experiencing fear or distrust in another, simply look for what is true about them, trusting and expecting that there is something divine in them that will unfold instead of seeing them as sources of potential threat, fear, hurt, etc. Harm cannot come your way when you are seeing clearly. In any situation, when you take the time to see God in another, how can there be fear or danger or threat? When you know that God is loving you and God is loving him or her, how can you be fearful or apprehensive?

"If you do not see clearly, look deeper until you see what God is being. You will see that God is being wholeness, beauty and perfection. It is a matter of persisting in looking deeper and further. Your brother or sister will benefit as much as you while you apply this extra effort and curiosity and willingness to see the more that is there in your brother or sister. Reality is always pressing to come forth and be experienced, and so it is not difficult to see what God is being in your brothers and sisters because it is already there waiting to be recognized and known by *you*. When looking at another and wondering what God is being, remind yourself that

God is being them, regardless of what they are expressing. In this way, you will help them become aware of their true nature, as expressions of Divine Love.

"In certain cases, where there is great resistance to seeing the truth, especially when there is much painful history in the relationship, instead of working at seeing the Christ in your brother, it may be easier to begin with the assumption that this is the truth about him. It will be easier than struggling to remove hurtful memories. To attempt to analyze or remove these memories may cause them to seem even more real than they need to be, causing unnecessary pain and suffering, none of which is required for awakening. In fact, pain, suffering, grief or struggle of any kind indicate a loss of peace, hence an impediment to awakening. The truth is available to you here, in the moment, now; it does not need to be excavated. If forgiveness seems impossible, if you cannot see the divine one in your brother or sister, assume that the Christ is there, that your brother or sister is already whole, a son or daughter of God. Simply accept what you are able to see at the moment while asking for help to see more as soon as you are ready. Your willingness to see the truth will eventually clear your vision, for this willingness is an expression of love, and love is the true substance of your being.

"Once committed to looking for what God is being in everyone and everything you encounter, you cannot but forgive, since to withhold forgiveness would mean delaying the full experience of Reality. If you are seeing a brother in any way but sinless, or innocent, you are practising judgment. To judge another is to look through the lens of the ego. It is to deny yourself the opportunity to experience Reality. To truly love someone is to abandon judgment, to be willing to look beyond and disregard the false definitions that are being acted out from the ego sense of self, to be willing to see the divine one that they are. It is to acknowledge their birthright, and this is the greatest gift you can make. At the same time, it is the greatest gift you can give yourself, for you are giving yourself the gift of true sight. To forgive is to invite real change and true healing."

The Search for True Love

Besides questions about career and life purpose, the subject of relationships is the next most common topic discussed with clients. After more than three decades of consultation practice with men and women of all ages, there is not much that surprises me except for one subject: love. I am still taken aback when I hear people describe the pain and anguish they allow themselves to experience over impossible and clearly unhealthy relationship scenarios, all in the name of "love." Love hurts, as the song goes. Some believe that it is necessary to experience pain to know love; to know light, one must first know darkness, and so they find value in suffering, which must be the most absurd justification for something that is completely false, even insane. How could a loving Father, the Source of Life, require that the one thing we need the most, love, be achieved through one moment of suffering of any kind? Clearly, the nature of love is gravely misunderstood.

But I love my partner; I would do anything for him, even if it hurts. I love her so much that I would die without her. He/she is the love of my life, they will say between sobs, sharing how the "love of their life" has run off with a new "love" interest. When the sobbing subsides, while wiping away their tears, they will turn to me and ask to know when the wandering partner will return. Really? Others will try to explain and justify why they continue to put up with abuse from the "love of their life." Many see themselves as the only one who can help the abusive partner because they "love" them and understand them so well. These lovesick souls are completely oblivious to the fact that what they are experiencing is anything but love. It is an ego-based game of guilt and manipulation, and it serves to prevent the one thing that could bring healing to both parties: love.

As we begin to look at these relationship situations from a new perspective, that of individuals playing a game of separation from our loving Source, it becomes clear that we choose our relationships because they validate some deeply engrained beliefs, some healthy and some unhealthy, about ourselves. If we were to change our beliefs, perhaps abandon the unhealthy ones for new definitions of ourselves, we might very well experience much healthier relationships. The truth is that we fear the emptiness and loneliness we would face if we abandoned our cherished false beliefs. We must be ready to question our beliefs and consider another way of being before real change can be experienced.

It is easy to love a partner with whom we have a positive, or more accurately, agreeable relationship. But true love is not determined by what another person does to us or for us, or how another person makes us feel. It is not founded on externals because that which is founded on externals is in the realm of separation, the kingdom of the ego. True love, by its very nature, is all-inclusive, so it is contrary to the idea of a private, independent, separate self. Love has the power to dissolve all boundaries no matter how unyielding they may appear. Since the ego sense of self can only survive in a climate of separation, it will not seek out, nurture or even entertain the idea of true love. Instead, it will focus on reinforcing and maintaining the boundaries of separation. The ego will cleverly protect itself against expressions of true love by confusing us with its very own special version—false love.

The false love of the ego serves to maintain boundaries by reinforcing beliefs, self-definitions, specialness and differences; it is based on bargains, negotiations, agreements and conditions. You recognize me as I want to be recognized, you see me as I choose to see myself, you help me reinforce and maintain my made-up definitions and beliefs about myself; you support the way I see the world, and I will return your "love" in kind. We are soulmates; together we are whole; we are a team; we were made for each other. Failure to comply with these relationship agreements almost inevitably leads to the suffering and grief of "heartbreak." While they may stir up some warm and fuzzy romantic feelings, the problem with relationships founded on separation is that they serve to uphold false beliefs, many of which are belittling, demeaning and even hateful.

The essential nature of the ego is fearful, defensive and adversarial, all traits that are at the root of the "love" of the special relationship. Being based on a lie, false love is vulnerable and must be defended. Motivated by a need for self-protection, it can lead to behaviour, actions and relationships that are inappropriate, unhealthy, unintelligent, unwise and simply not beneficial for all concerned. It generates negative emotions such as anxiety, fear, insecurity, jealousy, competitiveness and possessiveness. When the loss of the "love" of a special relationship results in feelings of grief, loneliness, hopelessness, misery, desperation or even the desire to end one's life, it is an indicator that the ego's boundaries have been disturbed. In such cases, the ego sense of self is feeling threatened and is at risk of being exposed for what it is—a fraud. What is not love is fear; incapable of knowing love, the ego can only generate fear. When fear is experienced, know that true love was not at the heart of the relationship.

We sing songs of love; we search the four corners of the world for it; we pine for it; we write poems about it; we set aside special days in its honour; we even claim that love is the answer, yet we don't choose it. Why is that? If love is the only true healer and if love is the answer to the suffering of humanity, why do we not choose love instead of hatred, resentment, divisiveness, competition, alienation, anger or any other emotion? The reason for refusing to choose what we claim to be the only valid answer is that we believe there is something more valuable to choose in its place. If we choose "not love" instead of love, it must mean that we value "not love" more than we value love. Why would we value anything other than love, when withholding love from another is to withhold that which we claim to desire most? It can only be that we still prefer to experience separation rather than true joining. It is not love that hurts, as so many of our stories and songs claim; it is the withholding of love that hurts.

Although love is the central message of many teachings, it is still not humanity's first choice. If all of humanity chose love over any other motivation, then many structures in our societies would crumble. In a culture of Oneness, greed and self-interest would no longer be sustained, and so everything would change. Love would require the complete acceptance of the divinity of each person we encounter. There is no room for separation in the presence of love. Being all-encompassing, as long as there is a continued and sustained desire to maintain separateness for the sake of personal gain and self-protection, love will not be chosen. While everything that is sought after and accomplished in the illusory world of separation is the result of tremendous effort, love fortunately does not need to be taught, cultivated or earned. It is there waiting to be experienced, since it is the substance of our Being. All that is needed is the willingness to make a different choice, the courage to open up our hearts and trust that this is the true path for the healing of humanity.

> The ego is certain that love is dangerous, and this is always its central teaching. It never PUTS it this way; on the contrary, everyone who believes that the ego is salvation is intensely engaged in the search for love. Yet the ego, though encouraging the search very actively, makes one proviso; do not FIND it. Its dictates, then, can be summed up simply as: "Seek and do NOT find." This is the one promise the ego holds out to you, and the one promise it will KEEP. (ACIM, Chap. 11, p. 265)

The one thing that is feared the most by the ego sense of self is true love, because love forgives, love does not see error, love is not blinded by lies, costumes, judgments and false definitions. True love sees the human condition for what it is—nothing more than a game of pretend. Love does not require punishment, penitence or absolution; love simply accepts, since it knows that nothing in Reality can be harmed. Most importantly, in the presence of true love, the ego sense of self ceases to be. It is what humanity truly needs. It is easy to understand that from the perspective of the ego, there is no motivation for choosing love over our current way of being.

True love can easily be recognized because it is unconditional, all-inclusive and unlimited. It is at the heart of the experience of true joining; it is inherent in the holy relationship. It is an expression of defencelessness and sees no need for boundaries. It knows that the brotherhood, the sisterhood, of man finds its greatest, most creative, most inspired expressions in its Oneness, in union. Love inspires the innate Intelligence that is available to the whole of creation and being complete, it cannot engender fear, sadness, possessiveness, jealousy, grief, distrust, hatred, anger, resentment, envy or loneliness. Being a natural expression of Being, love does not need to be enticed, solicited, earned, purchased, controlled, manipulated or coerced in any way. It simply needs to be allowed. True love feels good, safe, whole and overwhelmingly joyful. Love is wise; it understands the situation and will always inspire appropriate action. It is gentle and never causes harm. Love is firm and unwavering; it is not subject to the laws of insanity. Love is given freely and waits only to be accepted. Once accepted, love is complete.

> The life of the soul is not knowledge, it is love, since love is the act of the supreme faculty, the will, by which man is formally united to the final end of all his strivings—by which man becomes one with God. (Thomas Merton, *The Seven Storey Mountain*)

CHAPTER 7

Calls for Love

> Mistakes are FOR correction, and they call for nothing else. What calls for punishment must call for nothing. Every mistake MUST be a call for love. (ACIM, Chap. 19, p. 456)

A Call for Love

It may seem as though just changing how we see a brother couldn't possibly have any impact on our world, but such a shift has much greater significance than we realize. If we came to this faulty view of the world, and of ourselves, because we agreed that we wanted to experience separation from our Source, the only way to change the experience is to pull out of the agreement and be curious to see differently, to know the truth. Pulling out of the agreement opens the door to new experiences, usually surprisingly pleasant ones. When an ego-based invitation is ignored, the divine nature of each involved in the interaction is allowed expression. When we see that which is divine in another, we have seen without filters and definitions; we have seen with our right mind. Clearly then, it is in the interest of our goal of awakening to persist in seeing what is really there rather than remaining focused on what is seen within the limited human perspective, through the filters of judgment, memory, teaching and beliefs. By far the best place in which to practise this new way of seeing is in our everyday interactions with each other.

The Course makes it clear that there is only one kind of judgment that is valid and that is the capacity to distinguish or discern between two possible expressions: love or a call for love. Since we all share the same Source, everyone has the capacity to make that distinction. There are only two voices: the voice for truth or the voice of the ego, and only one is real. In all circumstances, we choose which will grab our attention. In any situation, regardless of the behaviour, a brother or sister is either calling for love or expressing love. This distinction can only be made when the mind is free of expectations, emotional reactions, false beliefs, memories, judgments, personal investment and, especially, the always ego-satisfying need to be right. In order to respond in the most appropriate way to whatever situation we are facing, there must be a deeply rooted desire to know the truth and the willingness to make the required change of perception to access this truth—the readiness to choose the miracle.

In relationships, as in all life situations, the first place to start is from peace, the necessary condition for being in our right mind, the only condition in which truth, the essence of which is love, can be known. It is also the state of mind that fosters the ability to listen to and hear guidance. Peace is our position of greatest strength, clarity, intelligence and wisdom. If we are experiencing a lack of peace, it is because we have accepted the ego's invitation to look through its filters and so we are incapable of true vision. In the absence of peace, we are more likely to fall into our false definitions of ourselves and of others and in the process forfeit our right to our divine integrity. The easiest way to ensure that we are in the best possible state of mind to interact with love and appropriateness is to check in with our guide before engaging. This is probably getting really annoying to read but keep in mind that it is only the ego sense of self that can experience annoyance. Independent thinking and action are ego-based; in partnership with guidance, we have a better chance of positioning ourselves in our right mind.

Besides not wanting us to join with our guide, the ego will not support peace, because it is the one condition in which it cannot thrive or even survive. Anything other than peace will lead to responses that lack the vision available to full conscious awareness, keeping us trapped in the game of separation, unable to know the truth of a given situation. Only peace can ensure clear vision, appropriate action, wisdom and ultimately healing. Know that if an encounter has cost you your peace, the price was too high. To lose peace is to lose access to full conscious awareness, a dear price to pay for a moment of insanity, no matter how seemingly satisfactory.

Most people have had at least one encounter that has caused some degree of pain or suffering. Absence of peace is common in special relationships, especially in long-standing relationships that are weighed down by years of painful baggage due to conflict. It is in those situations where it seems impossible to be at peace, the ones that stir up anxiety, fear, anger, resentment, frustration, impatience, regret, shame, guilt or any one of the ego's countless unholy responses, that we find our greatest learning opportunities. If, after an encounter with a brother or sister, we find that we are not at peace, it simply indicates that we have chosen drama instead; we have accepted an invitation from the ego. Loss of peace is always the result of a choice we have made; we are free to choose to be at peace, or we can choose to set it aside for something more exciting. How can we not love the brother or sister who has helped us recognize the choice we have made? How can we not be grateful for another opportunity to practise choosing another way? It is a peaceful mind that would see these as opportunities for taking one step closer to awakening.

> You do not realize how much you have misused your brothers by seeing them as sources of ego support. As a result, they witness TO the ego in your perception, and SEEM to provide reasons for not letting it go. Yet they are far stronger and much more compelling witnesses for the Holy Spirit. And they support His STRENGTH. It is, therefore, your choice whether they support the ego or the Holy Spirit in YOU. And you will know which you have chosen by THEIR reactions. (ACIM, Chap. 15, p. 352)

When we choose to see our brother or sister through the clear lens of our right mind, we break the agreement that supports the false structures they have established for themselves; we see the truth of who they are. In turn, when our brother sees us clearly, this gives us the courage to release our own false beliefs about ourselves.

In this way, we are each other's saviours. It is in making the commitment to see the truth that the miracle of clear sight will change the world. True vision—to take a moment to look into a brother's eyes and remember God—is a gift we give each other.

More often than not, our daily encounters with others are likely to be non-confrontational; they are likely to be peaceful, even pleasant. It is important to remember that the same shift of perspective applies here too. In fact, when people are behaving relatively well in the dream, there is little reason to wonder if there might be more to them than what our limited perspective allows us to see. Everything is fine, right? To limit our view of them to the role being played, no matter how harmless or even peaceful, is still an act of withholding because we are denying ourselves the experience of who and what they truly are as expressions of Divine Life. However, because there is little interference to true sight in these peaceful encounters, it takes very little effort to look into their eyes and remember God, thus allowing the divinity in them to be revealed. In this way, an ordinary encounter is transformed into a holy encounter, for only in the holiness of our right mind can we see the holiness of the other.

> To accept yourself as God created you cannot be arrogance because it is the DENIAL of arrogance. To accept your littleness IS arrogant because it means that you believe YOUR evaluation of yourself is TRUER than God's. (ACIM, Chap. 9, p. 219)

A Rare Love Story

Given the all-pervasive belief in unworthiness that is—and must be—sustained by the ego sense of self, it is understandable that the subject of "self-love" might generate some mild or even strong feelings of discomfort. Until we begin to release our faulty definitions about ourselves, we may not be ready to accept who we truly are as divine expressions of a loving, Infinite Life Source, deserving of perfect health and eternal happiness. Just the idea of seeing yourself as a son or daughter of God may cause a shudder or two.

Many have been taught that to think "highly" of oneself is arrogant and unacceptable, even a sin. *A Course in Miracles*, however, states clearly that to belittle oneself is arrogance, for it is the belittling of an expression of God. What is arrogant and cruel is to mistreat and to withhold love from a child of God.

If everything in existence is an expression of God, then each person—including you, including me—is also an expression of God. As sons and daughters of God, we should expect to be treated with the same kindness, dignity, respect and love that others are requiring from us. As long as we do not honour and respect ourselves as whole, divine expressions of the Infinite Life Source, as long as we believe ourselves to be small, insignificant, unholy, unworthy, screwed up, defective or lacking in any way, we will not believe ourselves to be deserving of love. If we do not believe that we are deserving of unconditional love, we are not likely to allow it into our life. If we do not honour and respect the integrity of our Being, others are likely to follow suit; we will accept invitations to engage in relationships with those who agree to uphold our beliefs. Relationships founded on the absence of wholeness serve to keep us from experiencing the Love that is our Source.

Although our self-definitions may be ill-founded, they are an integral part of how we see ourselves. They will affect how easily we will accept a new definition, especially one so radical that it dispels everything we believe to be true, one that suggests that we are expressions of a loving Father, beloved sons and daughters of God who could never do anything to anger their Father. Our readiness to abandon the ego-based denial of our true nature will determine our capacity to love and also our readiness to *be* loved. As we begin to drop the defences that keep us separate from everyone and everything else, our experience of love grows. This will likely require a giant leap of faith and trust that we are deserving of the experience.

When I point out a special quality or an outstanding positive trait to a client, it is not uncommon for them to express uneasiness, even embarrassment. Thank you, they say, clearly uncomfortable because I have invaded that private space where they keep their false beliefs about themselves secure and inviolable. To which I reply that

I am not intending to pay a compliment, rather I am simply stating a fact; simply shedding light on what is true about them. Many people have trouble seeing and acknowledging their qualities, being more comfortable with the faults and the flaws they are so busy addressing, maintaining and putting forth in the game. I can just see the old tape rolling in their eyes: How can I be a son or daughter of God when I am so defective? How could God possibly love someone like me? I'm such a screw-up; how could that which is divine ever love a total loser like *me*? However, all forms of Self-denial are nothing more than devious, self-protective ego distractions. How could a God of perfect love withhold love from any aspect of His creation, seemingly great or small?

Depending on the direction of the consultation, sometimes we will take the conversation a step further. To have an experience of who they are as Self rather than as ego sense of self, I may ask them to consider a radically different perspective. I invite them to contemplate the following: If everything in existence is of God, then *I* must be of God. If everything that God creates is like God, perfect and whole, then *I* must be perfect and whole. If I am experiencing anything less than my perfection, wholeness and health, then I must be experiencing a substitute version of what I am; something that is false; something that is not of God. That which is not of God can have no real effect and can simply be abandoned. If the nature of God is Love, then I must be loved by my Father/Mother or Source, regardless of what I may or may not have done, for true love must see beyond illusions.

I then ask the client if they have ever truly loved themselves. They may express how well they have managed despite all the obstacles they have faced, or they will bring up some of their accomplishments and worldly successes, or share how relatively happy they are with their life, at which point I will ask the question again. Have you ever loved yourself in the same way that you loved your son or daughter on the day they were born? If they do not have children, I may substitute with a puppy or kitten. To illustrate the point, I cross my arms and hug myself. How did you feel when you held your baby girl for the first time? Once they understand what I mean, I ask the next big question. Have you ever felt this way about yourself? They pause, sometimes teary-eyed at the memory of that experience of total love, and after some awkward hemming and hawing, astonished by the sudden revelation, they shrug and admit to never having truly done so.

I have yet to meet one person who has felt that kind of total, unconditional love for themselves, regardless of age, gender or life experience. To put them at ease, I share that, to my own surprise, I did not have that experience until the age of 58. Oh, true, I had loved my daughters unconditionally, but I had not truly loved myself, depriving them of a very important lesson. Imagine the ambivalence of the young soul who is loved by a parent who has never truly loved himself or herself. To this day, I remain surprised to learn just how rare are experiences of true self-love. No one has ever replied with a resounding "yes" to the simple question: Have you ever truly loved yourself? If love is an essential component of any relationship, how can we expect to be loved by another if we have not accepted love for ourselves? If we have not truly loved ourselves, how can we require that others treat us with dignity and the respect we deserve as divine expressions of our loving Father/Mother, Source?

How can we truly love another when we have not truly loved ourselves? The so-called love experienced between players in the game of separation must not be an expression of complete, true love, at least not until the love of oneself has been experienced and embraced as essential and healthy and totally appropriate. As love is the foundation of all holy relationships, to love oneself is essential for transforming special relationships into holy relationships. The love I offer another is the love I must first offer myself. I cannot love another unless and until I am ready to love myself. How can I be the presence of love if I have not accepted love for myself? How can I extend love when I do not know how it truly feels? And most importantly, if I have turned my back on the true Source of Love, how can I even claim to know love? How can I give love if I do not have firsthand knowledge of the infinite, healing nature of the love of the Father/Mother? The first love then must be the love

I accept for myself as a beloved child of God; only then can it be extended to others.

> Beyond the poor attraction of the special love relationship, and ALWAYS obscured by it, is the powerful attraction of the Father for His Son. There is no other love that can satisfy you, because there IS no other love. This is the ONLY love that is fully given and fully returned. Being complete, it asks nothing. Being wholly pure, everyone joined in it HAS everything. This is not the basis for ANY relationship in which the ego enters. For every relationship on which the ego embarks IS special. The ego establishes relationships only to GET something. And it would keep the giver bound to itself through guilt. (ACIM, Chap. 15, p. 363)

How to Respond to Calls for Love

If we have chosen to play the game of separation, it follows that we have also chosen our playmates. While we nurture those special relationships that will allow us to play a good game, it is those very relationships that can help us remove the blocks to our awakening. If we have chosen our relationships, these must be the relationships that offer the best opportunities for healing and, ultimately, for awakening. Before engaging in an encounter with another, whether it is a friend, a family member, a co-worker or just a stranger, it is always wise to be still an instant, choose peace and check in with guidance. Here we go with that guidance thing again! This is getting annoying, the ego will grumble. However, when we check in with our guide, we are taking a major step out of the dream. It is as though one of the children playing in the basement has decided to poke his head through the doorway at the top of the stairs for a brief conversation with his older sibling. Checking in is what brings us closer to our goal of awakening; it connects us with Reality.

While checking in is especially helpful in those encounters where conflict might be experienced, it is equally valuable in conflict-free encounters. Roles are roles, dreams are dreams, illusions are illusions; whether happy or sad, easy or difficult, they remain in the realm of the kingdom of the ego. To experience awakening, it is essential to reach out and take the hand of one who can show us the way Home. By joining, we are less likely to be blinded by judgment, memories and ego-based definitions, therefore more open to clear, intelligent, loving and appropriate responses. Besides, when reaching out to our guide, we feel accompanied, not alone, but more than that, we feel loved; being the presence of love, our guide is incapable of withholding love. We have nothing to lose by joining, only the faulty, limited ego perspective.

We seek out and attract relationships with those who will validate and sustain the beliefs about ourselves we wish to uphold. If we believe ourselves to be victims, we will attract those who are willing to play the role of victimizer. If we believe ourselves to be unworthy, we will attract into our lives people who will treat us as though we were worthless. If we believe ourselves to be vulnerable, we will attract those who will be willing to test our vulnerabilities. Our interactions reflect our ego-based beliefs, and these beliefs only hold sway in the game of separation. However, since these beliefs do not reflect who we truly are, we are not stuck with these interactions. At any given moment, we can abandon our beliefs. Once we accept that we are expressions of a divine Source, we will cease seeing ourselves as being vulnerable, and our special relationships can begin to heal.

It is important to remember that whatever we are experiencing, it is *never* about the other person. We are always responsible for our own experience. Our response, our reaction, how we feel is always a reflection of a choice we have made: peace or not peace, invulnerability or vulnerability, worthiness or unworthiness, our right mind or the tainted perception of the ego. At the same time, the other person involved in the equation is responsible for his or her own experience. If they lose their peace in response to something we have said or done, we can rest assured in knowing that their reaction is their responsibility, not ours. If we are able to accept this important premise, it will be easier to return to peace when we have allowed ourselves to accept an ego invitation for anything other than peace. Peace is a choice.

The following are answers to typical questions asked by clients. They are general in nature and can easily be adapted to a variety of circumstances. Keeping in mind that most people living on the planet at this time are not awake, it is pointless to blame, accuse, judge or be upset with their behaviour. It is understandable that their behaviour will be less than enlightened because they are proceeding from a limited, ego frame of reference. No matter the situation, our power always lies in choosing peace, our best ally is our guide, and our strength comes from loving ourselves enough to honour our integrity as divine sons and daughters of God. Taking the time to tune into these steps places us in an entirely different frame of reference, one that provides us with the opportunity to shift from the limited view of the dream to the all-encompassing perspective of Reality. To actively engage in this new perspective sets us on the path to awakening and it is our awakening that will contribute to the healing of humanity.

What can I do when someone is acting out or behaving inappropriately?

When a person behaves in a way that is not appropriate or in a way that does not reflect their divine being, it does not mean that we must accept their portrayal of themselves. Our function always remains to look for what God is being in them and to choose to be the presence of love. It is in this way that we will know our true Self. There is no need to acknowledge the inappropriate behaviour; in fact, to withhold a response, especially any form of ego-based response, can contribute toward its correction. In all circumstances, disregard takes the wind out of the ego's sails, while attention feeds it. From peace, we can then look beyond the role being played in the game and ask for help to see the divinity in our brother or sister. If appropriate, we may be guided to take specific action, especially in cases of imminent danger for those involved. Full conscious awareness does not mean lack of involvement; love is always intelligent and appropriate.

When it is difficult to see the divinity beyond the acting out, it can be helpful to imagine this person wearing an amusing costume, playing a lively role in a show. We would not be upset if we saw someone behaving in this way within the context of a play or a comedy show. The role they are playing or acting out in the human condition is also pretend. Although we may not like the particular role that the person is playing in the game, it is to our benefit to persist in looking for the son or daughter of God that they truly are, for it is then that our vision can be healed. Remember also that how you are seeing them is a reflection of your own beliefs; for example, if you see a threat, it reflects your belief in your vulnerability. Should you see a reason to be upset, no matter how justifiable, a decision for something other than peace has been made; in the absence of peace, only a limited perspective is available.

In some cases, it is best to simply walk away from a conflict situation. Peace needs never be forsaken for an ego invitation. It is always our right to refuse to engage or participate in any form of activity or encounter that pushes us beyond our ability to remain at peace. This is where our freedom resides: we are free to choose, always. This is where our true power resides: the power to say no to what does not respect the integrity of our Being. Peace is the required condition for awakening, it is our most valuable asset and should never be squandered senselessly; ego invitations are always senseless. Simply find an appropriate excuse to withdraw from the scene, even if it means fibbing a little in order to leave the room, or altogether end the meeting or encounter.

Those who find themselves in a disruptive environment on a daily basis may, after checking in with their guide, consider other employment or activities. Suffering and sacrifice will not pave the way to awakening. Suffering, sacrifice and guilt are fodder for the ego's game of littleness. Loving and honouring oneself is more important than complying with ego agreements when one is seeking full conscious awareness. Sometimes learning to say "no" and drawing a clear line is what is most appropriate. This is how the world begins to shift; by saying no to inappropriate encounters and engagements, eventually, they cease to be, since it takes two to sustain a special relationship.

What is the best way to help someone I care about?

This question is usually asked by caring and well-intentioned souls, sincerely desiring to be of help to their loved ones. It is important to remember to honour yourself when engaged in personal relationships because they are usually bound up with deeply rooted definitions and agreements. A good rule of thumb is the following: unless the person has asked for help, don't jump in. In other words, it is best to not assume that it is your place to get involved. Maybe you've "been there"; maybe you know better, but if the person is not yet ready for help, your involvement, no matter how caring, may be perceived as intrusive meddling. Your help may even be taken as an insult by that person who may be attempting to address the situation from their best knowing. If you jump in and offer help, chances are that you have judged the situation from your limited perspective; judgment is always contrary to love. Each person clings to those beliefs that define them in the moment, and these beliefs can only be released when we are ready to abandon them or when they are no longer suitable. To abandon beliefs too soon can generate fear and cause instability.

If you think a call for help has been made, remember to check in with guidance—there's that guidance thing again!—and wait to see if it is appropriate to offer help. When someone needs your help, they *will* find you. If you are unsure about the person's ability or willingness to ask for help, you may be guided to ask if they would like your help. You can always reassure them by saying that you remain available for whenever they need help. If there is the slightest hint of guilt, obligation or anything but peace, chances are that you are attempting to help from the perspective of the ego. When two play the game from the perspective of the ego, neither can rise to Reality.

Fortunately, as in all circumstances, there is always something we *can* do. It is up to us to correct the way in which we see our brother; it is not up to us to correct a brother's behaviour. Each person chooses to experience as much difficulty, suffering or challenge as he or she can tolerate; unless we are seeing with clear vision, we are likely to incorrectly evaluate the situation. Some people can tolerate a lot of drama, others much less. It is not up to us to judge how much is enough for another person. Each one attracts the circumstances that suit their role in the game. Our only function is to choose to see in a new way, to persist in seeing the divine one that they are, to look into their eyes and remember God. Our function is to choose peace so we can be the presence of love.

I feel bad for this person; they have had such a hard life. How can I help them?

To feel sorry for someone because they have had a hard life is actually neither kind nor loving; it tends to be condescending. It says that some are less deserving than others and have been given fewer opportunities in life. The hard truth is that each person chooses their storyline; each person has as much drama as they can tolerate. Everyone is a divine expression of the Life Source; everyone is deserving of experiencing wholeness, abundance, perfect health, peace and joy. To be experiencing anything less is to choose to accept less for oneself. The best way to help this person is to persist in seeing the wholeness in them, the divine Self that is covered over by the ego sense of self. When they are ready to see this about themselves, they may ask for your help in accepting it, if that is your purpose. As long as they are deriving some ego satisfaction from their suffering, they are not likely to accept your offer of help. Your function is to withhold judgment and be the presence of love.

How can I be with my friends when they don't think as I do or believe what I believe?

You can be with others and do normal activities and engage in conversation without agreeing with their beliefs. You can still remain at peace and be centred. If there is nothing appropriate for you to say, you don't say anything at all. You may have noticed that most of the time, they are not really waiting for your comments. They just like to express themselves. And sometimes that expression is loud and vocal and animated. This does not need to affect your peace. Your function is always to look for what God is being in them; this offers you an opportunity to heal your vision.

But, I tried to make them see, but they are just so stubborn!

Sometimes, those individuals who are the most vocal and intense about their opinions are the ones who are closest to breaking through a new boundary of conscious awareness. The more fearful a person is of letting go, the more tightly they will hang on. It is pointless to argue or attempt to convince someone who is standing firmly by their view, even if they are expressing a view that is clearly incorrect. Let them talk; that's probably all they need at this time. When ready to expand their vision, when they are ready to let go of their inaccurate beliefs, they may turn to you for help. Truth is not debated, it is experienced; love is not taught, it is felt.

Note that although you may have been guided to respond in a certain way today, it does not mean that the same response will be appropriate tomorrow or the day after. When the practice of joining with guidance has been adopted, each moment can be approached without fear, concern or worry as a new moment, which is how the Movement of Being is experienced. When joined, you are most likely to respond in the most appropriate way.

How to Handle Mistakes

Mistakes are not corrected from within a state of ignorance. They must be corrected from the perspective of the right mind. However, as individuals functioning in this world of dreams, we must at times deal with the consequences of our misguided actions. A common initial reaction is to berate ourselves for having acted poorly, or having acted without love, or having acted in a way that is inappropriate. Most likely, the so-called inappropriate action was taken without first having joined with guidance, therefore from a place of limited clarity. Love yourself enough to forgive yourself and move on. The Father will never hold anything against us; He simply waits for us to wake up to our true divine natures. When we remember to engage in the practice of joining with guidance, our actions are more likely to be beyond reproach. Guilt is never justified.

Even with the best of intentions, mistakes will be made. A common initial reaction is to berate ourselves for having acted in a way that is inappropriate for a person on a sincere spiritual quest, a feast for the ego whose only intention is to keep us away from peace. One day, I found myself drawn into a downward spiral right through the centre of the darkest recesses of my mind. Even though I thought I had replaced most of my faulty beliefs about myself, I came face-to-face with some deeply buried unsavoury beliefs I had accumulated since my youth. I saw all the mistakes I had made throughout my life, errors of judgment, my inability to successfully integrate into community and society, my inability to fit in, failed relationships, failed attempts to be normal and be accepted, and recently, my inability to awaken from the dream. My life was a long series of failed attempts at trying to be human, and in recent years, a series of failed attempts at trying to wake up.

For a few days, I felt as though I had dropped straight into hell. God was nowhere near. I was completely consumed by the overwhelming awareness of my failures, and there was no relief in sight. Unwilling to remain in this pit of darkness any longer than necessary, I engaged in simple activities that I enjoyed, peaceful activities like rearranging my clothes, switching out summer clothes for winter clothes, putting order into my pantry, things I could do easily, and without too much error. I did some cooking; I did manage to screw up a batch of tempeh, but it didn't matter. I would make errors. I felt like I was releasing a mountain of inner garbage, as if I was standing on the side of the road on garbage day, and it stank. This was hell. The absence of being in the presence of God is truly hell, and during that dark passage, God was nowhere in sight.

Finally, out of the desolation of this stumble into darkness, a small voice reached up, and suddenly, with the help of my Friend, I saw clearly. It was normal and natural to fail at being human because being human is not our normal condition; our natural condition is to be divine. To be anything less than divine can only lead to failure. Oh my God! I had failed in my attempts to be what I am not. This was a good thing, a very good thing. All that remained was to give myself permission to be what I truly am: whole, spirit, a thought in the Mind of God. All that was needed was to be curious, to explore what God is being in me in the moment.

I was also reminded that, since each person chooses their experience, we cannot hurt another person any more than another person can hurt us. If we believe we can be harmed or hurt in any way, it is because we believe we are vulnerable. Therefore, we have rejected the truth of our invulnerability, our wholeness, and we have identified with the ego. The one who chooses to experience vulnerability will see danger, conflict, disharmony and threat. The one who chooses to see Reality will see beyond the error to the call for love.

Those dark, demeaning beliefs about myself, and the mistakes I had made had always been there; I was aware of them, but this time I was actually ready to release them and accept a replacement, the truth about myself. This was a significant step forward; the old way of seeing myself and knowing myself was being undone; a new way of being was emerging. I knew that I would make more mistakes as I became familiar with this new way of being. In fact, making mistakes is inevitable, since the first mistake is to function independently from our Source. But now I had a new reference point toward which I could turn when I lost my centre. I would love myself enough to return to this new reference point: that I am essentially divine; you are essentially divine; we are essentially divine. And, of course, I would try to remember to join with my Friend all the time!

Breaking the Agreement

The following is a simple exercise for facilitating the healing of a relationship that has become entangled in the false definitions of the ego. Keeping in mind that special relationships are sustained by mutual agreements, to withdraw our agreement is to break the bonds of the special relationship. The relationship now becomes an opportunity for healing and becomes a holy relationship. There is only one condition for the success of this exercise, without which it will not work: One must be fully ready to release the agreement. This means no longer seeing the other through the filters of memory, beliefs, definitions and judgments. This means releasing whatever benefits one derives from the relationship, whether positive or negative. It means being ready to be in a new way with this person.

Find a quiet place to sit and meditate for a few minutes. This is an exercise that you will be practising on your own, in the absence of the other person. Since minds are joined, there is no need for the other person to be present for this exercise to be effective. In fact, to have the other present might distract you from the full clarity available when you are in the quiet centre of your mind. This exercise will, however, be facilitated in partnership with guidance, so it is most appropriate to invite your guide to join you.

Once peace has been established, imagine yourself going back in time, before you were born, to that moment where your souls made the initial agreement to journey together in the make-believe world of the ego. In this peaceful frame of mind, outside the confines of roles, definitions and memories of life in the game of separation, invite the other to join you. Imagine that you are pure spirit, soul or mind and that the other who has now joined you is also pure spirit, soul or mind.

You may begin by thanking the other for joining you in this exercise. Next, in your own words, clearly state your intention regarding the healing of the relationship. For example, you may let him or her know that you no longer wish to maintain an ego-based agreement. Thank them for having played along with you in your imaginary game of separation and for having provided you with an opportunity for learning. Let the other know that you are now releasing them from the agreement that binds you in the dream state and keeps the both of you from experiencing your divine wholeness. Without the false definitions and biases of your ego, what remains is the divine Self that God is being in your brother or sister. You may feel great relief and joy as false definitions are being released; with the blocks to the presence of love removed, true joining or communion can occur.

This is not an exercise that needs to be repeated; however, if you were not completely ready to release the agreement when you first did the exercise, it might be helpful to repeat it, as needed. All that is needed now is that you practise being with this person in a new way.

If you were truly ready to see this special relationship transformed into a holy relationship, you are likely to see evidence of this healing. While there is no need to tell the other person that you performed this exercise because it is never about the other person, you may be pleasantly surprised when he or she responds to you in a new way. This is evidence that minds are joined. This is evidence that every little miracle, every little shift in perception can contribute to the healing of humanity.

CHAPTER 8

The Purpose of the Body

The special relationship is totally without meaning without a body. And if you value it, you must ALSO value the body. And what you value you WILL keep. The special relationship is a device for limiting your self to a body, and for limiting your perception of others to THEIRS. (ACIM, Chap. 16, p. 394)

Making the Separation Real

Standing in front of the bathroom mirror in the morning, few would dispute the fact that they are anything other than a distinct individuality, residing in a physical body that originated with the joining of a sperm and an egg, endowed with conscious awareness that is centred somewhere in the grey matter located between the ears, and that they exist separately from everyone and everything else. Well, maybe not first thing in the morning, maybe after a coffee or two. However, we are now being taught that, by its very nature, the One Mind cannot engender any form of division, separation or independence. Furthermore, if we experience ourselves as being separate and independent from our Source, it is because we have chosen to experience something unnatural. While we may have chosen to have an experience of separation, Oneness has never been, and can never be divided, and so our experience as separate, distinct bodies is not an experience of the truth of who we are.

In the limited human condition, while intent on experiencing separation, the body serves to establish boundaries between self and non-self. Because separateness is not our true condition, we must constantly work at maintaining, nurturing and protecting the body. While we believe ourselves to be encased in physical bodies, we must shield ourselves from countless seemingly very real dangers, from the elements to disease and even from each other. Because the idea of a separate body is just that, an idea, and it is not our reality, it is vulnerable to one thing—the truth. The truth always remains that we are expressions of the Infinite Life Source, all is happening in the One Mind and no real experience outside of the One Mind is possible. To divert our attention from the truth, the ego, or the separated sense of self, will distract us with constant bodily concerns, from fear for our life to an endless array of sensory distractions.

While our attention is focused on tending to the body's needs and ensuring our material security and comfort, we are validating our status of independence and making the thought of separation real. The more preoccupied we are with these needs, the less we are available to ponder the fact that we are spirit, that we are not just bodies, that we are expressions of an infinitely unfolding divine Source. We reward ourselves for our successful existence as separate entities by catering to the physical senses. We punish ourselves for the guilt of having apparently accomplished the impossible feat of separation from the Infinite Source by accepting to suffer pain and illness. Whether through reward or punishment, the purpose is always the same: to prove, sustain and protect the illusion of separation.

The Course tells us that we are free, that we are not bodies and that we are as God created us—as God is being us now. We are thoughts in the Mind of God and that which is of God, or the Divine Source, is like Itself, forever whole, perfect and always new. When I first encountered this bold new perspective, I had trouble accepting its full implications. How could I be whole, never mind perfect, as God created me, or as God was being me now? In fact, it was hard to accept that God had anything to do with who I was *now*. As confusing as it was, the idea that creation is ongoing was the one element of this new perspective that brought hope. If creation is occurring now and if it is constantly renewing itself, then no physical condition is permanent or irreversible, and any physical condition can instantaneously be healed.

I had been experiencing ongoing pain in my shoulders and neck, a common syndrome for those who have spent decades working at a computer. I had questions about the physical body, or physical reality, which still seemed very real to me. If we are thought, and everything is thought, then what happens to physical reality when we wake up? The following are snippets of insight from my Friend gathered over a period of several months on the subject of the body, illness and health.

"To think and be convinced that you are a body is the result of the habit of thinking that you are a body. To release yourself from this habit, you simply create a new habit of looking for the truth of what you are—as spirit, mind, thought—the body simply being the tangible and visible expression of what God is being in you. Before you can fully experience this, you need to practise turning your attention inward. You will not see the truth by looking out into the world.

"Everything that appears to happen, everything you think you see and feel is actually occurring in the mind. There is only mind. Physical expression is an experience of the mind. When the mind is changed, physical expression is changed. Physical expression is simply one way of experiencing what is in the mind. Physical expression does not necessarily disappear; what disappears is your limited perception of what is, of creation, of life being eternally new. Physical expression is there as one means of experiencing creation. Physical expression changes as creation changes and is renewed moment by moment. When you awaken, physical expression becomes a means by which you can recognize and identify what God is being. This is simply one aspect of the expression of creation. It is not all there is to be experienced.

"The purpose of the body is to identify you in the limited human experiment. Having a body does not diminish having spirit, or *you* as spirit. Having a body does not change you as spirit or modify you in any way. However, identifying solely with the body or the physical representation of you and forgetting that you are spirit is the problem. Not that you are a body, but that you have forgotten that you are spirit. Spirit has never been modified in any way. Spirit remains where it has always been. You have never stopped being spirit. You simply have mistakenly identified solely with the physical expression of who you are.

"The body is like the packaging of the product. It takes a marketing team or committee to develop an image or a package for a product. But the packaging, the box in which the product comes, for example, the wireless speaker you purchased, is not the wireless speaker. The packaging is designed to sell the product. Your body is designed to represent you. If you believe that you are spirit, that you are whole, as God created you, the body will be whole. There is no need for it to be otherwise.

"If the marketing committee decides to misrepresent the product, to misidentify the product on the packaging, you, as a consumer, will be dissatisfied with the product. If your body serves to identify you, you should be dissatisfied with it as the representation of you if it is ill, broken, expressing pain or is not functioning properly. If it is not whole and perfect, it cannot be representing the *real* you."

Despite these words of wisdom, I continued to experience discomfort. There was crunching and cracking when I moved and stretched, no doubt a symbol of the crumbling of my ancient beliefs, as well as ongoing tension in my upper back and shoulders. My contemplation now was focused on the fact that, if all that exists is what God is creating, and what God creates is perfect and whole, then I must be perfect and whole, including the physical expression of what God created as me. If I perceive anything other than my perfection and wholeness, then it must mean that I am clinging to an image that is a replacement, or a substitute, for the true image of what God created, or of what God is creating in the moment.

All that remained was for me to release my beliefs, my false perception of what God created as me, so that I could experience the physical evidence of the perfection of what God is being in me. Illness is not of God. When God is allowed to be, then illness has no place and cannot be sustained. I was beginning to see that the greatest discomfort was the result of my persistence in identifying with a self other than what God is being in me. Maintaining this false self requires a tremendous expenditure of energy. It limits and excludes everything that God is expressing right now, all of which is new, not defined by me, but above all, out of my control. The only way to get rid of tension (for example, the physical tension I felt in my back) was to give up maintaining and nurturing this false self. I gathered further insights from my Friend.

"There is lingering guilt that is experienced as ongoing pain in the back and shoulders and arms, which appears as discomfort from too many years at the computer. It is a convenient setup. And then there is guilt compounded by the inability to experience healing. There is always only one cause of discomfort or lack of ease of any kind, and that is the decision to resist the expression of your wholeness.

"Your health is guaranteed by God. It is given to you because it is God's will for you. Anything less, any discomfort, is the result of you resisting your health, your wholeness; it is you wanting to, for a while, be less than what you truly are. Relinquish your resistance to your wholeness. Let your health come to you; it is your natural condition. Your health is not under your control. What is under your control is your illness, your clinging to something other than what you are: whole, spirit, as God created you. Let go of that limited version of yourself. Embrace your wholeness. To focus on fixing the pain or healing is to focus in the wrong direction. Focus on the wholeness that is your true inheritance. Put your attention there instead. The healing will occur naturally.

"The body is a physical representation of you, it is not the entire you, it is a third-dimensional representation of who you are. You have simply hijacked this limited level of expression and made it the entire identification of you. You are always, and have always been, an expression in the Mind of God; you have never been just a body.

"God is being you regardless of the definitions that you have given about who and what you are. Give up these definitions, and you will know what God is being now. All that is required to experience what God is being is to be curious. Be curious to experience what God is being by withdrawing your attention from what God is *not* being. The Father does not heal or take away your pain. He waits patiently, holding your wholeness in His hands. He waits for you to give up your ideas of pain and anything less than perfect wholeness. He waits for *you* to welcome your wholeness.

"Only one step remains, and that is to accept that, at every instant, God is being you and God is being me. Stop thinking or trying to understand that. Just allow yourself to feel it, yield to it. That's all that matters. God is being you; God is being me."

I understood then that my focus should be on health, not illness; that I should be curious to experience it, to know what the Father has in store for me. Health and wholeness should be experienced physically, visibly, tangibly, even if the experience is in the mind. That should be the experience. Not an experience of pain or discomfort or physical disharmony of any kind. Since there will always be an experience, whether correct or mistaken, why should it not be a joyful, comfortable experience of wholeness?

Healing My Relationship with the Body

But who is this or what is this that I am if not a body? When I was young, one day I let myself imagine if the "me" I thought I was would be affected or altered in any way if the body were changed. For example, if I cut off one of my legs, would I still be the same person? I reflected on the hypothetical situation a moment and concluded that yes, I'd still be me. If I cut off the other leg, would I still be the same person? Again, I concluded that I would be the same person who was observing these events, although I may not appear the same in the eyes of others. What if I were to cut off an arm? What if I were to cut off the other arm? Would the "me" be any different? No, I would still be me, which led me to conclude that I must not be just a body; I must be something more than a body, something that could not be altered like a body.

A few years ago, it came to me, as though a warning of things to come, that the body would be my last big lesson. I found this to be an unwelcome revelation since at the time I still believed that one day I would be free of the burden of being in a body. Being in a body had not always been a comfortable experience for me. There were times when I felt that my spirit was trapped in a dark, confining world of form with no way out. My experience had always been a far cry from being my Self as spirit, or mind, let alone an expression of the Father, or anything even remotely divine. Clearly, I would have to learn to see the body in a different way.

One evening, in the winter of 2013, an opportunity for this new learning arose. I had been watching television, relaxed in an armchair with my legs stretched out on the ottoman. When the show ended, I switched off the television and turned to get up. As I placed my foot on the floor, something snapped at the top of my leg, as though a nerve had been pulled out of its socket. A jolt of what I could only describe as sizzling electric current shot down the inside of my leg to the sole of my foot. I had never felt anything like this before; it was uncomfortable and, most of all, frightening. I stood motionless, fearful that I might have irreparably damaged a nerve, afraid of aggravating the situation if I moved. To my great relief, after a couple of minutes, the sensation dissipated. I shook out my leg and, with no further sensation, simply forgot about it, assuming that all had fallen back into place.

It was a couple of weeks later when, during the night as I turned over in bed, I experienced another nerve shock. At that time I had been deep in the overwhelming business of selling the house—not my favourite kind of business at all. Clearly, the last thing I needed was a health issue. *Not now!* I said. *I don't need this now!* Apparently, the firmness of my declaration had sufficient power to reach whatever part of my mind had rulership over the body, for the situation once again resolved itself, at least until I had sold the house and settled into the condo.

If only I had worded my declaration differently. If only I had said *not ever!* But I hadn't. Several months later, bit by bit I began to experience mild nerve firings, especially while walking. As the months passed and the situation did not resolve itself, I learned to manage the discomfort by moving my body more cautiously. Running, leaping, taking long steps were out of the question, as they were certain to trigger nerve shots. I walked more slowly and I especially avoided crossing the street when there was the slightest chance that I might have to run to make the light. Although this did not constitute a healing, at least in this way I managed to contain the situation. The healing would come, although I was growing a bit concerned by how long it was taking.

Given everything I knew about mind, body, spirit and healing, I could have found interesting correlations and meaning in this situation. I was susceptible to nerve damage because of my Aquarius ascendant, I was fearful of moving forward into my awakening and so on. I could have gotten a lot of distracting mileage out of this issue, but I had no interest in focusing on the illness. I wanted to focus on the healing; I wanted an experience of healing. I was ready to let the false beliefs about myself rise to the surface so they could be released and so I could experience my wholeness. To remain focused on healing, I listened to the Raj material that related to healing and the body, especially the meditations. I asked my Friend to shed light on the meaning of discomfort.

"All discomfort is the Soul's cry for attention. It says look here, what you are doing is not appropriate. The best way to approach any situation of discomfort is to back out of it, find inner peace, be still and listen. To attempt to rectify an uncomfortable situation from the level of the uncomfortable situation is a waste of time and energy."

At night, before going to sleep, I pondered long and hard this new way of seeing myself. I am not a body, I am spirit; I am a thought in the Mind of God. Still, my experience was that I was a body. My body was simply a momentary, temporary encasement for the idea of me. It was that which represented me in the moment, as was my bed, the blankets that kept me warm, the room that was my nightly refuge and the condo that offered me shelter. In my prayers, as I joined with the Father and yielded into the Oneness, I began to try to experience rather than try to understand what all of this meant. My bed is an idea; my body is an idea; I am an idea. It all served a purpose.

The bed served the purpose of holding me while I slept. Yet, it was just an idea. My body was an idea, and if it wasn't only matter, if it wasn't just form, if I was only experiencing it that way in my mind, then it could change. All I could do was appreciate it, love it for the function it served in identifying me in the moment. I was long past attempting to understand all of this. In fact, I did not want to understand. I wanted the full experience. I let myself experience the love that was the form that appeared to be me, as well as the love that was the bed that supported me, the blankets that kept me warm, the room that was my refuge and the condo that was my place of shelter. All of it was love.

I continued to contemplate the idea that I am a thought in the Mind of God, that perhaps this physical experience does not constitute all of reality, but rather reality perceived in a limited way. Although I may be represented by a body and I may feel locked into my experience of this physical representation, it is not the totality of who or what I am. I am a thought in the Mind of God. If wholeness is our natural condition, then pain must be a form of resistance to our natural condition. Pain is resistance to wholeness. Illness is resistance to wholeness. The quickest way to get rid of pain is to abandon resisting wholeness, to welcome and allow wholeness.

Healing would require the abandonment of my definition of myself as being trapped in a broken, damaged body. If I were to accept the radical new view of matter as an idea in the Mind of God, the Creator or the Infinite Life Principle, that would mean the end of everything as I knew it. That would mean the end of what the ego had on me: identification with a body that is vulnerable and susceptible to pain, injury, illness and death. Without the limited perception of what I am as a body, the ego's rule would come to an end.

Despite my sincere contemplations on another way of being, the condition worsened. In the summer and fall of the following year, I scheduled appointments with doctors in the hope of getting a proper diagnosis. Mostly baffled by my description of the condition, the doctors sent me for a bunch of irrelevant tests, from gynecological (don't ask; I suspect that we didn't have the same version of *Gray's Anatomy*) to blood and cholesterol. A neuropathy might very well be permanent, was one doctor's best conclusion. As odd as this may sound, the diagnosis of permanence struck a chord; it was something with which I could work. Instead of causing fear, it inspired me to continue to look for my wholeness. Illness could not be permanent, since what God is being is always in movement, always moving toward wholeness. Besides, I had learned to move in ways that did not aggravate the situation much.

However, by the third winter, the situation worsened to the point where I feared turning over in bed at night or stepping out of bed in the morning or even just getting up to answer the phone. I had long given up my daily walks and basically turned into a recluse. Here I was with all this wonderful knowledge about bodies and healing, about being a divine expression of God, about being whole and perfect in reality, yet I was stuck with a condition that had grown intolerable and was likely permanent. My Friend had offered much support and insights, yet my healing remained beyond reach. I couldn't help thinking that I was an unbearably slow learner, adding a bitter dose of unhealthy and unnecessary guilt, shame and frustration to the mix.

One day, I put it all together. The body and I are one; the body is a divine expression, and I need to love it as I love myself, as God loves me. Although it is not all of what I am, I would need to embrace my body and allow love to infuse every single cell until there was absolutely no room for illness. I could not hate an aspect of myself and expect to awaken or even to live gracefully. To awaken would necessarily involve healing. In the middle of this realization, my Friend reminded me that I needed to trust the body, to trust that it could reflect divine wisdom and that it had the ability to heal itself. I also needed to be patient with its healing.

I had to believe that my Self was all there was of me and I deserved nothing less than the full experience of my wholeness. That was the only approach that would work for this healing. This would require total and complete acceptance of the Love that is the Source of all life, faith in my body's ability to return to its perfect wholeness and trust that this is what would be expressed. I was seeing how I needed to embrace this body, the form that represented me, and it occurred to me that I had never really liked this bodily representation of me. I had never really liked this body with all its faults, and now it was time to trust it and to love it so that I could experience its healing and wholeness.

With these bold new ideas about my relationship with my body filling my head, I decided to test my readiness to accept them. While the approach I took would probably not get medical approval, I had the full inner certainty that it would be appropriate for me, given my level of knowledge and faith in the body's innate ability to heal itself. I knew it would work. Besides, I was sick and tired of being sick; there was no way I would spend the remainder of my life catering to a disability.

One cold winter day, having suffered enough nerve firings to light up my condo for a year, I decided to face this annoying and debilitating condition head on. Really, I'd had enough. I had been focusing on the illness, catering to its calls, limiting my movements out of fear of its outcries. I deserved to experience my wholeness. If illness was not permanent because it was not an expression of truth, then wholeness was the only true alternative.

That snowy morning, I put on my snow pants and jacket and headed out for a walk. It was time to break out of this crippling ailment. With each step I took as I locked the condo door and headed out to the elevator, fire shot down the inside of my leg, and each time I said, "No! There is wholeness in my body, and this is what I want to experience." I kept walking. Fire shot down my leg with every long step I took, and each time I said, "No! I deserve to experience wholeness." After several steps in the crisp winter air, I relaxed into my walk and placed all of my attention on the wholeness of my body, its true condition.

By the end of that first thirty-minute walk, the nerve firings had considerably subsided. I continued with my walks every day that week and, as I did so, the sensations continued to diminish. Whenever I experienced a nerve firing, I repeated firmly, "No! I deserve to experience my wholeness." The condition diminished as the weeks turned into months, until I experienced only occasional, very mild sensations. That's much better, I told myself, pleased with my body's ability to heal itself. All I needed was to exercise a little patience and it would all go away, in time.

CHAPTER 9

More Than a Body

A sick body does not make any SENSE. It COULD not make sense because sickness is not what the body is FOR. Sickness is meaningful only if the two basic premises on which the ego's interpretation of the body rests are true. Specifically, these are that the body is for attack, and that you ARE a body. Without these premises, sickness is completely inconceivable. (ACIM, Chap. 8, p. 193)

More Lessons from the Body

It would seem that I needed to learn more from the body, for the following winter I experienced an adverse reaction to an antibiotic I had been prescribed. I was to take two tablets a day for ten days for an infection I had contracted a couple of months earlier. Over the first several days, I experienced a number of odd sensations, from dizziness to loss of appetite and, most unusual, frozen feet. My feet were so cold I had to wear thermal socks to bed. The sensations seemed to be disconnected, coming in waves, with periods of relative normalcy in between. On the seventh day, I experienced an unusual loss of energy, so much so that I felt the need to apologize to my client because I had not been feeling one hundred percent during the consultation. Actually, I felt as though I was functioning at about half my normal physical strength.

That Friday night, when it came time to take the first dose of the eighth day, I had a feeling that I should not continue with the prescribed full course of ten days. Since this was the second round of antibiotics for a urinary tract infection that was proving to be persistent and might have been on its way to developing into a more serious problem, I wanted to make certain that it was dealt with sooner rather than later. Besides, I didn't relish the idea of another visit to the doctor and another round of tests. Of course, being that I am stubborn in nature, despite my faint, though still present, *better* sense, I decided to take that next dose. I knew better than to not listen to my inner voice, no matter how distant it seemed, still I chose to use stubborn will instead of quiet listening. I was determined to take the medication as prescribed right through to the tenth day. I'm still not sure if I wanted to prove the doctor wrong or to heal my body; all I know is that I didn't listen to the still, small voice.

Just before sunrise, when I came to get out of bed to go for a pee, I instantly realized that I had made the wrong choice in taking that dose. I had lost so much muscle strength that I had to use both hands to hold myself up against the walls as I made my way to the bathroom. Of course, I lost bladder control on the way, and forget about reaching my intended target, I simply did not have the strength to make that happen. In shock and, honestly, frightened out of my wits, I cleaned up as best I could, grabbed a clean set of pyjamas and made my way back to bed. Too weak to do anything else, I spent that day sleeping and drinking as much water and juice as I could. The poison needed to be flushed out of my system. When I realized that a whole other set of muscles could become disabled if I took another dose, even possibly leading to my death, I decided not to continue with the prescribed medication; since no new reactions had presented themselves, I set aside the idea of calling 911. I would rest, pray and heal.

Besides being scared half to death, I was upset with myself for having brought illness into my experience. Again! Although the nerve issue was much better, it was not yet one hundred percent healed; and now this persistent infection. My healing was taking far longer than it should. I felt lost and alone, in a dark hole. What was I doing wrong? I prayed for guidance and for healing. I think my brain had been affected by the medication because I had difficulty hearing guidance. It wasn't until later that Saturday evening that, once again, I asked for help. In the quiet darkness of my room, I listened and waited. In a matter of minutes, I sensed the presence of my Friend. Reaching for the recorder I kept on the dresser next to the bed, I listened intently, and recorded.

"Let go, let go into the Mind of God. Know that you are *mind*. Let go into the healing arms of God, into the truth of what you really are."

I began to let go and let God while my Friend repeated gently, "let go, let go, let go." This time I sensed very clearly that he was sitting next to my bed. I felt his loving presence so strongly that I cried. I may have been at death's door, but I felt completely safe and loved and so close to God. In the quiet, in the dark, with my Friend sitting by my side, I felt no fear. I knew that if I were to die, which might have happened had I taken that next dose, I would have been just fine. In fact, I would have been more than fine. I felt closer to God than I had ever felt. It was a feeling that I never wanted to lose. I was loved; I was safe; I was more content than I had ever been in my life.

When it occurred to me that, as I healed and got back into my worldly activities, this feeling of closeness to God would most likely fade away, I was disappointed. I wanted to hold onto this incredible feeling of all-encompassing love and safety; I wanted to melt into it, to disappear into it forever. There was nothing in this world that could draw me away from this overwhelming sense of peace. I let myself fall into the Arms of God, enjoying every second of complete and infinite loving peace, clinging to it for as long as possible.

As I lay there, motionless, enveloped in blissful peace and contentment, I began to sense the presence of several healing helpers hovering around me. I sensed their love and their clear intent for my healing. In the dark, in the eyes of my mind, I saw the form of my physical body disappear. In its place, there appeared tiny oddly shaped lights of various soft colours. I somehow knew that this was "me" as light. It was a beautiful experience, and for a few moments I knew that I was beautiful. My body would take the time that it needed to heal or, more precisely, I would take the time that I needed to heal. But as the blissful experience faded, I was once again faced with my slow recovery; I had not been healed in an instant.

"Take advantage of this time of illness in which you have no interest in food or any other sensory experience to focus more on the experience of being from *mind* rather than from body. The reason it seems to be taking so long is due to the habit of engaging in sensory bodily experiences."

This request to practise being from mind rather than from body was not difficult since all I could do was lie in bed. However, while lying awake with no energy to do anything, my mind wandered. Besides being slow to experience healing, I was upset with myself for having made no real progress toward awakening. All these years—decades even—all this study and here I was, experiencing one illness after another, and no more awake than I was when I began my journey decades ago. Once again, I grabbed the recorder.

"The problem," my Friend pointed out, "is that you are trying to understand the process, or trying to understand the experience. Awakening is not going to be an experience achieved through understanding. It is going to be an experience that feels like something, it will feel like love; it will be far greater than anything you could possibly imagine. So to try to understand your way to enlightenment is really a waste of time and energy, and actually an impediment to the awakening experience. It is a distraction. It is simply going to slow it down.

"In order to experience immediate or instantaneous healing, you must be free of any resistance to your wholeness, your perfection or your divine heritage. You cannot just ask God to heal your body. God will not heal your body. God will heal your mind because it is your mind that is the source of the problem with the body, *your* misperception of the body, the perception of anything other than your perfection. Illness is misperceived truth, a distortion of perfection; it is not real; it has no foundation in Reality. It seems real only to those who experience the limited frame of reference of the body and the world. It is not real to those who experience the full range of what it is to be from mind.

CHAPTER 9 · MORE THAN A BODY

"This is why it is so important that you practise constantly being from mind, as opposed to being from a body. It is a good opportunity for you to practise this now while you are not overly distracted by sensory experiences."

There was much for me to ponder, learn and digest over the next several hours. The challenge for me became clear. It was how to integrate such a radical teaching while being in the world. Being a radically minded individual by nature, this teaching already appealed to me. But how was I to integrate this new view in a normal world at a steady, comfortable, normal, acceptable pace? I had no mundane or worldly goals or ambitions. My only ambition was for awakening. And now I saw that even this seemingly noble ambition was a problem. I needed to relinquish the impatience for awakening and simply allow the process to happen. I would not be able to understand the process nor understand the experience, at least not at first. I could not conceive of what it was going to be like because it was so far beyond what was being experienced by the bodily senses. Awakening could not be easily explained, at least not in a way that would be intellectually satisfying.

"A simple desire to know God is all that is needed," my Friend added. "Anything stronger or more intense will be a distraction. Peace is the condition; to desire peacefully is the ideal condition."

I questioned why my faith seemed to have failed so completely. I had faith in being the daughter of God, in being in the presence of God, and yet I had still gotten sick. My Friend pointed out that my faith was great, yes, but it was still largely intellectual. It wasn't yet total. It was from the heart, yes, but it wasn't yet complete. I just needed to let go a little more of any thoughts, objections, ideas or beliefs to the contrary. While I lay there in the dark, waiting for my body to become whole, I simply let myself fall once again into the loving arms of God. I let myself—all of myself—every cell of my body, fall into that Love; I let go and trusted completely in the healing, in my wholeness; I did not question it or doubt it. I let go, let go, let go into the Love of God.

A little later that night, my Friend explained that God does not test our faith by throwing challenges our way. However, the Holy

Spirit, our right mind, can use these situations as opportunities to help us learn; it can turn them to our advantage, as the Course says. The lesson here was that my faith needed a little bit more expansion. It wasn't that I was doing anything wrong but that I needed to do a little bit more of what was right, which was to have faith and yield to the Father. What a relief to hear that I was doing something right. I only needed to let go and let God. If I wasn't feeling one hundred percent yet, I just needed to let go a little bit more. The body is not to be feared; it is simply what God being *me* looks and feels like here, in the world of form.

I wanted to know then what God being me in Reality was like. I was shown that my true Self would be known by love, by feeling, that it could not be understood intellectually. I would have to set aside the desire to understand and simply be desirous of knowing it, and it would feel good because love can only feel good, and love can only be good, whole and healing.

Much was released in those hours spent with my Friend and with God and the healing helpers; so much relief came over me. I felt so much joy that I could barely contain myself. Finally, I took a deep breath, let go, let God and slipped into a deep healing sleep. When I woke up that Sunday morning, I had an urge for scrambled eggs, which was unusual since I had been eating mostly plant-based foods for a number of years. It seemed that my body needed eggs to help with recovery, and I was okay with that. However, still weak from the reaction to the antibiotics, plus not having eaten much in a few days, I couldn't see myself making it to the elevator, let alone the grocery store, even though it was just across the street. Just before nine that morning, the phone rang. A friend wanted to know if she could drop by and pick up the keys to her daughter's condo, on my floor. "Of course," I said. "Oh, and would you mind picking up a dozen organic eggs for me on the way over?"

By the end of the following week, I was back to normal. I did require another round of antibiotics but this time, I was prescribed the old-fashioned variety, not a new-fangled designer drug. The infection was completely cleared up in a matter of days. From what I learned over the next couple of weeks, I was very fortunate to have experienced such a rapid recovery. Others had not fared as well, suffering various long-lasting or even permanent paralysis. One neighbour told me of an acquaintance who had died from the same medication. By the sound of it, I had recovered very rapidly.

I had learned that the facing of challenges such as extreme situations or hurdles is a point in which a shift can be experienced. This is when our spirit or our awareness can grow. The situations themselves are not God-given challenges. I know that now. In other words, a challenge is a point of growth, a point where we can no longer be where we were before, where we have reached a threshold of being in another way. But the challenges are not necessary for growth either. Where God would have us be, no challenges are required. They happen to be very helpful because they are usually accompanied by some degree of discomfort, and discomfort can lead to questioning, to looking for another way and, best of all, to giving up control and confidence in what we know. At that point of letting go, we are more open to accepting a different perspective.

After getting up one morning, I returned to bed for a few extra minutes, just to reconnect, to be in the presence of God. My Friend pointed out that I will always be in the presence of God if I look for God in everything and in everyone that I encounter throughout the day. I am always encountering something, every minute of every hour of my waking day. So in remembering to look for what God is being, I will never lose that presence of God.

On another occasion, in my morning prayer I asked the Father to help me be in the world today. I was contemplating the idea that I am a thought in the Mind of God, expressed as spirit, seen as form. How can I stay in that place where I am spirit, or how can I remember that I am spirit? How can I remember to be there more frequently, even all the time?

"Simply come back to the thought, remind yourself that you are spirit, that you are a thought in the Mind of God. You tend to condemn yourself for forgetting that. Also, you tend to analyze too much and think about how you got away from the truth. Simply place your attention on the truth. There is no need to analyze the error, the mistake, or to wonder how you moved away from the truth. Again, simply love yourself enough to take the time to pay attention, be present and remind yourself that you are spirit, a thought in the Mind of God being expressed as you. Remind yourself; stop analyzing and simply remind yourself.

"Stop *thinking* and remind yourself. Once you begin to think about what to do, where to be, where to go, then you have lost that thought that you are spirit. You can continue to do and be and go about your daily activities while remembering that you are an expression of the Mind of God. Simply remind yourself; introduce the new habit of remembering that you are spirit; replace the old habit of forgetting that you are spirit and thinking that you are only a body."

As I stretched and prepared to get out of bed, I was reminded of the ongoing pains in my shoulders and upper back.

"The discomfort you are experiencing in your body, in your neck, and in your shoulders and arms only appear to be a logical and an unavoidable consequence of being in a body and having spent thirty years working at a computer, as you like to say. But that is when you view yourself as body. When you view yourself as spirit, none of this matters. As you begin to view yourself as spirit, the beliefs you have about how you experience life as body will fade, and healing can then occur.

"If you constantly remind yourself that you are spirit, there will be a point where you will know this, and believe it and have more confidence in it. Once you fully appreciate that your true Self is spirit, your form on this level can take on whatever *form* is appropriate. Once you know that you are spirit, whole, perfect and forever being new, there is no justification for seeing or experiencing a form that is not equally whole, perfect and forever being new. And so there is no place for illness or discomfort of any kind.

"When your attention is distracted by a physical pain, like the sore in your mouth right now, just remember to give equal time to the thought that we just talked about, that you are spirit. Go back into that experience of being spirit. Balance out your attention so that your attention will not always be on the body. You have simply veered off centre and brought your attention to the body. Bring your attention back to the centre, where you are mind, where you are thought, where you are spirit. Just bring it back, direct it back gently. Do not berate or condemn yourself for being so slow and ignorant, as you usually do. Love yourself; be gentle with yourself, the same as you would with a child, the same as you did with your daughters. When you do bring your attention back to the thought that you are mind, that you are spirit, let it be more than a thought. Take a moment and let it be experienced. What is this experience of being thought or mind? Take the time, pause, be with it, don't just think about it, *be* with it."

And so I did. I dabbed some honey on the cold sore and did a little morning yoga. The cold sore disappeared that day, and the tension in my back was relieved some. It was a start.

Memory versus Knowing

While I was working on this chapter, a friend shared her own experience of healing. It was such a beautiful and simple expression of truth that I had to let her know. In response, she graciously offered her story for inclusion in this chapter. Since our shared experiences contribute to the healing of the whole of humanity, I am only too happy to share it here. Thank you, Pam.

Recently, I sent out an excerpt that I called "Memory vs. Knowing." And I have been having some experiences with this lately.

Memory: In the past I have experienced swollen salivary glands. It starts out with pain when I try to eat something, even when it is something that is soft and doesn't need any heavy chewing.

So when the condition returned, my first thought went back into my memory of how painful it could get and how I would have to go to the doctor or ER to get it healed. So I asked the Father, "What is really going on here?" The next thing I knew I was thinking that it was the "ego whispering in my ear." So I said, "Ego, shut up!"

The Knowing: Then I decided to sit quietly and talk with the Father. So I reminded my body that it was God's Perfection and every cell of my body was filled with the Father's Love and Perfection.

Then I thanked the Father for His, Her Love and Perfection that is all there is to my body.

The next time I took a bite of food, I again felt a little pain in those glands. Before taking another bite, I once again thanked the Father for His, Her Perfect Love that fills every cell in my body. I did it again with the next bite. And then it was gone, and I was able to eat the rest of my dinner in Peace without pain.

I felt this lesson was a lesson in not giving away our authority, which we always give away to the ego. The only memory we need to use is to remember to talk with the Father/Mother, God, Holy Spirit, etc. and remind ourselves of Who we Are, which is the Father's Love and Perfection that fills all our cells and our body temple. We are the Father's Mind. We Know this, only, with all of our human conditioning, we have forgotten it. So there is a need for us to at least remember this, and all is well.

> Your body is part and parcel of what you truly Are. It is the visibility and tangibility of your Individuality. It has, therefore, a divine or real function, and that is to render visible the presence of your Individuality. It therefore knows how to do it perfectly. This is important. *It knows how to do this perfectly.*
>
> The self-doubt and the fear around the body, the distrust of the body, the wondering what *it* is going to do next, as though *it* had a mind of its own, the hate that eventually grows relative to the body—all of these factors get in the way of your experiencing the body's inherent and natural tendency and objective to render your Individuality visible and tangible. (*Conversations with Raj*, July–August 1988)

CHAPTER 10

Breaking the Isolation

You dream of isolation BECAUSE your eyes are closed. You do not SEE your brothers, and in the darkness you cannot look upon the light you gave to them. (ACIM, Chap. 12, p. 296)

Walking with God

Back in 2012, when I was guided to put my house up for sale and make an offer on a condo, I understood that this move, besides making sense financially and practically, would also contribute to the breaking of the isolation I had enjoyed for much of my life. A year earlier, I had been guided to leave my MP3 player behind when I went out on my daily walks and then to adopt some unusual new practices, at least unusual for an inveterate isolator such as myself. For as far back as I can remember, probably since the invention of the first Walkman, my walking gear always included a headset through which I would listen to music, and then, in later years, lectures. Now I was being asked to abandon this long-familiar practice and adopt a very different one. My Friend asked me to walk with God; be fully present in the moment; be curious to see what God is being in everything and everyone I encounter. I was being invited to bring my attention outside my comfort zone and to look with new eyes.

I must admit that when I stepped out the door that first headset-free day, I felt a little naked. However, as I adopted this new practice, I came to understand that the music and the lectures I had surrounded myself with throughout all these years had acted as a buffer of sorts, a form of insulation between me and the world around me. Since all is an expression of God, I had effectively cut myself off from everything beyond the words and music that filled my awareness. I had set up a limiting structure around myself that, while perhaps allowing me to feel safe and comfortable, nonetheless prevented me from experiencing the more that was available to be experienced. My isolation had held back all that could be experienced in the awakened state I so desired.

It wasn't long before I was comfortable with my newly adopted defencelessness and I quickly grew to appreciate my walking meditations. There was so much beauty in the flowers and trees and the songs of the birds and the shifting shapes of the clouds in the sky, all of which I had only been partially aware while engrossed in a lecture or a piece of music. But it seemed that more was required, because next I was nudged to take it a step further. *Smile*, my Friend said. Now I was being asked to do something that was completely out of character for me: I was to smile at strangers. *Really?* To smile at the strangers I encountered while walking along the main boulevard—now there was a major step in opening up to what God was being in my brothers and sisters.

However, having begun to listen to my guide and having reaped notable benefits for having done so, I did as suggested. Since this smiling business was going to make me appear like a complete nut case, I thought I'd throw in a *hello, bonjour* or maybe a *hey* for good measure; I might as well go all out. I half-expected that passersby would ignore me, or maybe look at me funny, taking me for an escapee from the loony bin. Instead, I was surprised to discover how easy it was for people to respond with a smile or a hello of their own, no matter their age, gender or skin colour. In those brief exchanges, I truly began to see God in the people I encountered, in my brothers and sisters, which was not only a revealing experience but also a beautiful gift. There were divine souls hidden behind the cloaks and forms they wore, and these souls were waiting to be acknowledged. In my willingness and desire to see, I was showered with glimpses of their innate beauty.

Sometime after having adopted this practice, I caught a video on the Internet of an upbeat song by Victor Wooten, an artist with whom I was unfamiliar. Intrigued by the title of the song "I Saw God," I watched in amazement as Victor walked down a busy street, took notice of passersby and sang "I Saw God the other day, just walking down the street." The lyrics of the song so appropriately reflected my walking meditation experiences that I had to laugh and also shed a couple of tears of profound joy, fully appreciating the evidence of the miracle that was the awakening of humanity. Truly, awakening begins when we look into our brother's eyes and remember God.

> A MAJOR contribution of miracles is their strength in releasing man from his misplaced sense of isolation, deprivation and lack. (ACIM, Chap. 1, p. 11)

The Cave-in-Tibet Mentality

While I was pondering my reclusive nature, my Friend shared the following: "If you perceive yourself as being alone or isolated, it is because you have chosen to see yourself as different from your brothers. This has been a pattern in your life and has led to your being marginalized by the uniqueness or the differentness of your beliefs and ideas. You forget that ideas are not the truth; *being* is the truth."

It is true that most of my life I had skirted the margins of "normal" society, and I had been quite comfortable in my state of isolation. Sometimes I would look out at the world and say, only half jokingly, "I want to go live in a tree." I didn't have the stuff that makes people ambitious and driven for success; I had no interest in the accumulation of material things. Besides, I was too sensitive to hustle, compete and fight my way up the ladder of success, and I generally avoided conflict like the plague. I had no interest in the complicated and often quite messy life struggle that many engaged in with great passion and excitement. Being minimally involved and remaining as much as possible on the fringe was safe and comfortable. I also came to understand that my seeming sensitivity to the world outside or my hesitation or lack of enthusiasm for participating in the world was actually a response to the ego's suggestion that I was vulnerable, that there is danger and that I could be harmed.

Over the years, I had become a typical seeker—shrouded in spiritual isolation, with minimal involvement in the world, one foot in and one foot out, always ready to leave. When I was in my teens, I had picked up bits of memories of lifetimes spent as a monk, which made a lot of sense, given my deep longing for the simple life, for peace and quiet, as well as my lifelong spiritual pursuit. I came to refer to this need for isolation as the "cave-in-Tibet" mentality. From what I have seen in consultation, this tendency toward isolation, at times expressed as engagement in a spiritual pursuit or affiliation with a religious or metaphysical group, seems to be common among those who are particularly sensitive or averse to the hustle and bustle of everyday life. Many individuals have adopted a spiritual path after having suffered extreme difficulties and so have abandoned drama for something more peaceful or at least, something tolerable.

"In my defenselessness my safety lies." (ACIM, Lesson 153)

Enlightened Engagement

One of the most important lessons I learned as I was breaking out of my comfortable isolation was that I am a member of humanity, a part of the wholeness of creation, and since this wholeness is all-encompassing and infinite, there is nowhere else really to be. Every person on the planet is our brother, our sister, a child of God; together, either we contribute to the limited human experience or we nurture the healing of humanity. The nature of the contribution we make always remains our choice. Each is as valuable and as deserving of love as the other; no one is more special than another is; no one is more holy than another is. If life cannot be divided, then all of the experiences of humanity belong to every human. This means that all expressions of the Infinite Life Source are connected and shared by all.

While being sensitive may drive a person to pursue a spiritual path, it does not mean that having a thick skin or being comfortable in the world precludes one from awakening. One is not more capable or deserving than the other; the miracle—the shift in perception—is available to each and every individual at any moment. Over-sensitivity does perhaps incline a person to seek out another way simply because it very often leads to feelings of discomfort, but it does not guarantee or ensure awakening or enlightenment. In other words, sensitivity has no bearing on awakening.

At the same time, it does not mean that one who is seeking full conscious awareness cannot find a place in the world that is appropriate and allows them to contribute to the healing of humanity. A person's ability or inability to deal with situations, encounters or conflicts in the world has no bearing on their ability to shift their perception or to be from a state of greater conscious awareness. Threat, vulnerability and the need for self-protection are founded on fear, the lifeblood of the ego. It is an attempt to prove that we are bodies, capable of being harmed, with limited life expectancy rather than expressions of the Infinite Mind, therefore invulnerable, infinite and unlimited. As long as there is a belief in vulnerability, and this belief leads to hesitation, or even refusal to participate in the world, a decision has been made to listen to the ego sense of self. Ultimately, participation in the world will do more for our awakening than remaining in isolation, because it will help diffuse this unfounded belief.

If awakening does not happen alone or in isolation, it is also true that awakening does not require a special environment. Any form of special group affiliation, whether spiritual, social, cultural or economic, that distinguishes and separates us from each other is part of the problem. It is a way of sustaining and maintaining separation and it can never lead to healing, or an experience of wholeness. By its very nature, Oneness cannot engender separateness. Again, if we are experiencing separateness, it is the result of a choice we are making.

No matter the justification, the practice of separation from the whole is actually a selfish practice. To exclude oneself from the whole is to withhold what God, the Infinite Life Source, is being in us. As a result, our brothers and sisters cannot benefit from our divine expression. It is an act of withholding love, and generates an unnatural, eventually uncomfortable, condition. To limit interaction with the world also prevents us from experiencing what God is being in our brothers and sisters, and so it delays our own awakening. To remain apart from the whole is contrary to the nature of Oneness, which is safe, harmonious, intelligent, supportive and all-inclusive.

Engagement allows for the full expression of our divinity, and so it is the best possible gift we can make. It also promotes the experience of joining, which, in turn, contributes to the healing of the belief in separation—the root cause of every problem experienced in the human condition. Awakening happens when we practise shifting our attention here, in the trenches, in the world, with our brothers and sisters, in this place in which we have agreed to play a game. Our participation in ordinary, everyday activities is essential not only to the full experience of our awakening, but also to the healing of humanity.

We Travel Together

Decades ago, I used to take the commuter train to school and, later, to work. Back in the day, passengers sat quietly reading their newspapers or the latest novel. No one spoke to each other; no one ever spoke to me, probably because of the tattered copy of Thomas Merton's *Seven Storey Mountain* on my lap, which in itself was probably a valid deterrent to making conversation. What can you say to displaced monk? Everyone quietly "respected" the other's privacy. When I was on the train recently, I couldn't help but notice that I was the only passenger not glued to a smartphone; I have a stupid phone, which I hardly ever use. When I go out, I like to be present with whomever and whatever I encounter.

I thought of Montreal, my home for over half a century, and what a wonderful city it is: multicultural, diverse and beautiful. Then I thought, how much greater it would be if we were to do something really bold and daring—if we were to drop the barriers that keep us apart, the barriers that keep us from experiencing the love that is our true nature, the love that we are. What if we were to look up and actually see the person next to us on the bus or the train, or the person ahead of us in line waiting to order that first morning coffee? What if we cared enough to turn to each other and we said, hello, bonjour, hi…

But it is not everyone who is eager to smile back and connect with a stranger. Now and then, I encounter an individual who looks away before I even have a chance to smile or say hello. At first, I felt a twinge of rejection, but then I began to sense their sadness or sometimes their profound anxiety and worry and so, with love, I respected their need for isolation. Why would someone turn away from a friendly smile or a hello? My Friend explained that there is great fear in accepting joining, love or kindness from anyone, let alone a stranger. It requires dropping one's cherished barriers, releasing fears and accepting one's worth, and for many people, this is not a comfortable experience, since these beliefs form the foundation of our self-definitions. However, love is kind and intelligent, and so from the quiet centre within, we will be shown the appropriate way to look at, connect with and thereby acknowledge the other's divine Self without causing undue discomfort.

Of course, there are those times when we come across someone who appears to be behaving in a way that is not particularly enlightened. However, this did not mean that the person's wholeness, or divine Self as God is being them, does not exist; it only means that they are not expressing it at the moment. I remind myself that just because I have not seen wholeness in a brother or sister, it does not mean that they are defective; it only means that *my vision* is temporarily defective. To persist in looking for and desiring to see what is really there instead of remaining distracted by an ego outburst will facilitate the healing of vision and will promote awakening.

You taught yourself the most unnatural habit of NOT communicating with your Creator. Yet you remain in close communication with Him, and with everything that is within Him, as it is within yourself. UNLEARN isolation through His loving guidance, and learn of all the happy communication that you have thrown away but could not lose. (ACIM, Chap. 13, p. 323)

Abandoning the Cave

In the winter of 2016, after having regained my health, I returned to my search for a good story to read and picked up a copy of a contemporary novel that had been highly recommended by a friend, also an author. It is the story about a group of individuals from various spiritual and religious traditions who have been invited to travel to Tibet to share their knowledge with a young Tibetan monk. Although the storyline did not quite flow in the direction I was looking for, it had a surprisingly powerful, if indirect, impact on me. Apparently, it is just what I needed in order to free myself of some long-standing, deeply rooted beliefs. I have since come to the conclusion that miracles often happen in the most unusual and unexpected manner.

At the start of the novel, the main characters first meet while on a airplane heading to a remote location in the mountains of Tibet. While none of the passengers knows exactly why they have been gathered together for this unusual excursion, they take the time to become acquainted and share views and beliefs from their respective religions and spiritual teachings. After a long and difficult three-day journey, the heroes of the story arrive within view of their destination, an ancient monastery, tucked high up on a rocky mountain ledge. To my surprise, at this point I began to cry; I cried so hard that I thought I was going to split in half. What struck me was that I saw these people going "home" while I remained here, in a comfortable Montreal suburb, living a life that was furthest away from the life of a monk in a Tibetan monastery. They were going home, and I was not. I cried and I cried, releasing a lifetime of longing—lifetimes of attachment to the monastic life. When finally I ran out of tears, I took a long, deep breath and turned my attention to my Friend. *Okay, it's done. I'm finished; the isolation, the cave-in-Tibet mentality has finally been released. I'm free.* And I took another deep, healing breath.

Whenever I'm in need of support or encouragement, or confirmation that I have seen clearly or understood correctly, or clarification of an issue that is causing confusion or doubt, something comes to meet this need, usually within a day or so, sometimes even within minutes. Shortly after having wiped away my tears of liberation, I checked my e-mail and activity on my social media page. I noticed a link to a brief talk by Canadian actor Jim Carrey entitled "Spiritual Awakening Raising Consciousness." Although I knew next to nothing about Jim Carrey, I had the feeling that I should check it out.

In this brief talk, he describes an exquisite experience of expanded awareness in which he knew without a doubt that he was a part of something far greater than the self he knew himself to be. He goes on to say that ever since that day, he's been trying to get back there. I had to join in his laughter at his predicament. An experience of closeness to Truth—being in the presence of God—is never forgotten. After having had a taste, it is an experience one wants again, but it must be desired above any other experience. I thanked the Father for sending me Jim's uplifting story. Awakening is happening around the world, even in Canada, in all walks of life, even for actors! One does not need to be a Tibetan monk or an especially holy person or live in a cave in order to experience awakening. All that is needed is the desire to wake up and the willingness to allow it to happen.

I saw how, throughout my life, I had used this cave-in-Tibet mentality as a way of establishing a boundary between myself and everyone else. I had been a lost monk in a female body in the Western world, different from everyone in my surroundings and unable to fit in. It had been a clever way in which my ego sense of self had maintained isolation and separation, the very thing that was preventing me from experiencing wholeness and oneness with all of my brothers and sisters. It was time to release this belief about myself—a false belief—sustained over lifetimes perhaps, yet a false belief nonetheless. Anything that sustains separation, differentness and isolation can only contribute to unhappiness, even if it is separation by means of being a monk or spiritual seeker.

While I was working on the early chapters of this book, I had an experience during which I remembered the moment I decided to incarnate in this life. I heard myself say clearly, *Okay, I'll go back one more time.* At that moment, I fully accepted where I was, and I knew that I was where it was appropriate for me to be. After settling into my new life, free of my ancient desire to be anywhere else but in the moment, I received another little sign from God indicating that it was perfectly normal for me to be here in this world exactly where I was. The Saturday afternoon following my "Tibetan release," I heard a gentle knock on my condo door. It was a young man who lived upstairs with whom I had shared a few plant-based recipes.

"I'm feeling quite anxious," he said, standing at my door, looking distressed and uncertain. "Would you be able to teach me to meditate?"

It took a moment or two for me to grasp the full meaning of his request. Okay; now I really knew I was in the right place.

"Of course I can show you how to meditate." I immediately ushered him into the living room to my meditation chair. Once he was comfortably seated, I pressed Play on the CD player; a meditation CD was already cued up and ready to go. With simple instructions, I led him into a deep meditation.

Yes, indeed, there is a place in creation for all of God's children, even displaced Tibetan monks.

CHAPTER 11

A New Frontier for Humanity

Child of God, you were created to create the good, the beautiful, and the holy. Do not lose sight of this. (ACIM, Chap. 1, p. 19)

Nice and Easy

What is this desire to awaken? I have often wondered if I might be going crazy—talking to God, checking in with my *Friend*. What is it that drives someone to engage in such strange practices? I could just let it go, live a good life like everyone else. That would be easy. However, once touched by the presence of God, nothing measures up, and so it becomes difficult to remain oblivious to our divine birthright. Why should we settle for an insignificant morsel of infinite Life when all of it is available to us now? Together we could be having the most glorious experience of everything that life has to offer, a life of unbounded abundance, wholeness, perfect health, beauty and harmony. It seems like a no-brainer. Who would *not* want this experience? To settle for anything less is to deny—no, *dishonour*—our true Selves as expressions of the Source of Life, as sons and daughters of God.

One thing is certain about this crazy desire to wake up: it cannot be ego-derived. To awaken is to embrace the Self and in so doing the ego is abandoned. However, although the desire to experience full conscious awareness is certainly a promising sign, as long as there remains an ego sense of self lurking in the shadows of the mind, vigilance will be required. As far as the ego is concerned, all is fair game, including this noble desire, and since its survival is at stake, it will use whatever it can to keep us from this pursuit.

Everyone has quirks of character, those unique traits and behaviours that distinguish us from each other. One of mine happens to be occasional impatience, as is indicated by my strong 14/5 numerology signature. While our quirks may make for interesting personality distinctions, they make for fine ego distractions. Since we slip into these behaviours and responses mostly automatically, with little conscious awareness, the ego can easily slip in unnoticed and have its way with us. To add to this insight into my personality, my Friend reminded me—as always, with infinite patience, as though teaching by example—that, for awakening to occur, I would need to be patient with myself. All that is required is to desire it above all else. It would come in time, by itself, because it is my natural condition; it is *our* natural condition. Anything less than an experience of full conscious awareness requires effort and even struggle. Because being asleep is not natural, it eventually grows uncomfortable and is bound to be released. In time, we come to the realization that we no longer want to put effort into being what we are not. Awakening is a simple shift from the limited perspective of being in a body in a world of form to the broader, fuller perspective of being from Mind.

Given what I perceived as my annoyingly slow progress on what was supposed to be a journey without distance and my increasing curiosity about what more can be experienced in Reality, I remained a bit impatient when it came to the subject of waking up. However, while being impatient to wake up may seem like a worthy state of mind, it still has the effect of chipping away at peace, as well as drawing attention away from what God is being in the moment. Therefore, being impatient, even to wake up, should be addressed as another distraction, a clever delaying tactic courtesy of the ego, which, by now, had clearly gotten wind of this soul's fervent intent. Impatience also implies a lack of trust. If I lack trust in my unfolding, it will seem like a lengthy and difficult process. If I trust that my unfolding is natural and inevitable and simply allow it to occur, it will flow much more gracefully. Furthermore, in my impatience, I am withholding love for myself, which weakens my resolve.

Still, there had been ignited in me such a profound desire to experience my wholeness that I desired to wake up more than I desired anything else in life. I had an unshakable sense that there was more going on than met the eye, and I was determined to find out what it was. I was ready to let go of the illusory sense of self and embrace my true Self. Why was it taking such a long time? Again, my Friend was there to help. "Waking up seems to be taking a long time because you are hesitant to give up these definitions of yourself, or this personality that you are familiar with, for fear that there will be nothing to replace it. Also, to have a desire of any kind, including the desire to wake up—no matter how sane it might be—implies a lack, and lack is not possible in Reality. You want something you don't have. This will inevitably involve a pursuit, an active, wilful pursuit of the fulfillment of this desire. Even though it is in the right direction, it is still an activity that is contrary to the quiet mindfulness that is needed for awakening. Awakening, which is natural, does not need to be worked at or reached for, in any way. It is simply allowed. So it is that even the pursuit of awakening ultimately needs to be abandoned."

Message received, loud and clear. I must trust that this return to wholeness will occur regardless of the seeming obscurity in which I find myself. The only thing standing in the way of awakening is the belief that awakening takes time or that I am not worthy of experiencing my full divine Self. Picking up on the metaphor of the group of children playing in the basement, my Friend added this point: "If this can make you feel any better, remember that when you check in with me, you are reaching out to that place of greater awareness, out of your current level of ignorance. When any of you check in with your guides, it is as though the child is taking a break from his game and actually connecting with an older sibling, one who has grown up—one who is awake. The child knows where to go when he is done playing games." At least by checking in with my Friend, I was doing something right.

Adventurous Soul

Sometimes help is offered in unusual, even fun, ways. In my case, messages come via the song titles that scroll across my television screen; I like to listen to the classical and smooth jazz stations on my cable network. For example, while I was writing the section on how to talk about God in the first chapter of this book, I walked into the living room just in time to catch the title of the song that was playing, "Conversation with God." Another time, while describing to a client the benefits of joining with guidance, "If You Need a Friend" played softly in the background. I had to chuckle when, one day, while I was pondering my impatience about this foolish pursuit, I turned to the television and noticed the title of the song playing on the smooth jazz station: "Adventurous Soul." Okay. Thank you. That's much better than impatient fool.

Despite my occasional slips of impatience, I was experiencing more joy and a deeper sense of peace. Yet, I still felt pulled or divided, as though lost in a sort of nowhere land between the world I once knew and a new world that seemed foreign. My Friend responded in this way: "If you are feeling pulled or divided, as you say, it is because you still have an investment in both directions or in being in the world as well as in waking up. Also, in your case, it is because you still doubt your ability to awaken. Note that those times when you have felt divided is when you have spent time with others in the world, and you have done so on *their* level and have forgotten to join. You have looked through the eyes of the ego: with judgment, memory, conditioning, expectations, that is, within the parameters of the dream; you have forgotten to look with new eyes. This is why it is so important to be constantly partnered with your guide. It is not a journey you can pursue alone.

"You are learning how to be in the world in a new way, how to be *in* the world and not *of* the world. Again, this requires faith and a desire to be in a new way that is greater than the desire to be accepted by others; it also requires that you remain joined with me. It requires that you not care how others will perceive you. You do not need to worry about anything when you are joined with me and are at peace; you will always be appropriate."

Given everything I had learned, as an "adventurous soul," I felt that for every step forward, I was taking three steps back. My Friend helped out, once again. "It is not that you are taking any steps back; it is only that when you go back to the old way, it is becoming less and less acceptable, less and less satisfactory. Each step forward means less interest in going back. So you are not going back; you are going forward. With each step forward, you are experiencing more of what is truly good in Life, so going back has less appeal. The old way of looking and being becomes less fulfilling and less satisfying and that is absolutely normal. It is a sign of growing sanity, not insanity, as you may think. It may not be normal in the eyes of the world, but the world as you see it in the limited form is not normal; you know this already.

"Love yourself enough to continue taking those steps forward, even if they seem small or are not as frequent as you would like. They will become bigger, and they will be more frequent; going back will be less frequent, and it will have less of an effect on you. The joy from the forward steps will remain with you and wipe out the lack of joy or the unfulfilling sense you feel when you seem to take a step back. It's not really a step back: it's simply you, momentarily turning your attention to the old way.

"Because fear or a sense of loss or resistance are encountered, it does not mean that you are doing anything wrong; quite the contrary. It is an indication that you are breaking loose from the hold or the clutches of the ego sense of self. You do not need to go any faster than is comfortable. This feeling of loss is not an indicator of failure. You are experiencing a period of adjustment. That's all. Nor is it surprising or unusual to have this experience, given that being on the path toward Home marks the end of the ego sense of self, that with which you have been familiar for such a long time."

Once again, I thanked my Friend. Those were encouraging words for a restless, adventurous soul. As often happens with new learning, my Friend's words were really brought home when I was least expecting it, in this case, while out shopping for a new pair of boots for my daily walks. It was cold but sunny as I headed out to catch the 10:10 train, normal February weather for Montreal. Chances were slim that I would find a pair of snow boots so late in the season—I have long, narrow feet, and all the stores I had checked out were out of stock in my size. The only place left was Tony's Shoes, and their website was down. My Friend had given the excursion a thumbs up, hinting that it might be good for me to break up my daily routine and stretch my boundaries a little. Even if I didn't find what I needed, I looked forward to the trek into town.

My boots had seen better days, and not wanting to walk through downtown Montreal on a weekday with heavy snow boots oozing of glue and patched up with electrical tape, I decided to wear a pair of low dress boots. While my lower limbs may have looked elegant, my footing on snow and ice was uncertain. Despite the heavy salting, there was snow, water and ice on the roads and sidewalks. Because my dress boots had very little grip, I needed to tread cautiously, which meant making frequent glances toward the ground. But I was in no rush; I was at peace; I was accompanied by my Friend.

On one of those downward glances, while stepping carefully over a patch of ice on the sidewalk, instead of seeing my long black winter coat, in its place, I saw the folds of a long, pale ochre garment. I recognized it as the rough fabric of a monk's robe I had worn in a different time, a life in which I had experienced profound peace. Immediately I was moved to tears—joyful, grateful tears of the Soul. I resisted the tears, not wanting to draw attention and not wanting to walk into the store with puffy eyes. I breathed deeply and let myself be filled with the joy, the peace and the love of this wonderful piece of my past.

Once in the store, I attended to the business of explaining to the salesman what I was looking for. Several minutes later, he brought out three pairs of boots; the third one was exactly what I needed. Having found the perfect pair of boots, I decided to break them in by walking back to the train instead of taking the subway. As I stepped out onto the icy sidewalk wearing my warm, comfortable, non-skid boots, I relaxed and the image of the robe returned. A deep sense of relief came over me, as though I had recovered a lost part of myself.

The sensation of wholeness extended outward until I felt as though I were a part of everything and everyone: I was the fellow walking ahead of me, the storefront I walked by, the sidewalk and the snow and the water and the beautiful blue sky above. Tears welled up again as I realized that I felt more whole than I had ever felt in my life. I had found a lost aspect of my Self. I saw that nothing Real can ever be lost. Since every one of us is an expression of the Divine Source of Life, every one of us is made up of perfect light, energy and love and, no matter how shattered or broken or lost we seem, our wholeness remains always available to us. As we abandon our limited definitions about ourselves, we make the way clear for the recovery of our divine wholeness.

What Will It Take to Wake Up?

If the message of *A Course in Miracles* seems difficult to understand, perhaps it is because it is doing its job. The Course is designed to undo the ego structures so that the miracle—a shift in perception—can be experienced. The ego needs to understand so that it can control, handle, manipulate and manage the dream life to play a better game, maintain the distraction and thus protect its illusory existence. The Self employs full conscious awareness to know, sense, recognize and appreciate Reality—what God is being in the moment—without the need for understanding. Because being awake is natural, it is not dependent on understanding nor is it the result of research, analysis, study or learning. Understanding comes naturally, as needed, in moments of clarity, when we are ready to step over a new threshold of awareness. Understanding always serves to make the next step easy, graceful and very often joyful. While the ego is busy attempting to understand so it can have better control in the dream, awakening is occurring naturally, and a new Knowing is being revealed.

Maybe awakening is not happening quickly, maybe it is stirring up fear, confusion or another form of discomfort, or maybe the whole idea just seems too far-fetched. Since to be awake is our natural condition, perhaps we should give ourselves the benefit of the doubt and just stick to it. Clearly, the familiar way of life in the limited human condition—experiencing repeated birth, life and death cycles—is not acceptable for souls meant to experience infinite life, love, perfection, joy, creativity and wholeness. Awakening has never been withdrawn, diminished or made inaccessible. If it seems out of reach, it is only because we have momentarily become tangled up in the game and have lost sight of the truth. There must be another way, and that other way requires that we be willing to stop, be quiet, listen and allow for a shift in perception.

Motivation for awakening will not be found in the illusory dream state sustained by the ego sense of self. Because this is a new experience at this time for humanity, corroboration is not likely to be found in the world either. The motivation to experience full conscious awareness can only be found within, where the true Self resides. To kick-start the process, awakening must be desired above all else. Once the desire has taken root, it too will be released and replaced with a simple allowing. It may be helpful to remember that being awake is natural, while being asleep is not. If a stirring for this journey is being experienced, it is a call of the true Self that is catching our attention.

As long as awareness is limited to an autonomous self-protecting ego sense of self, we cannot know the true meaning of everything we encounter on a daily basis, nor can we know our true purpose in life. Once we begin to grow restless to experience the full movement of creation that is unfolding through and around us, our experience expands. This desire for a greater experience of Reality is natural, since full conscious awareness is part of our essential nature. Like the boys and girls playing in the basement, there comes a time when curiosity moves us to explore other possibilities. When the children grow tired of their make-believe games and decide to venture beyond their playroom, they make the most startling discovery: they are not children at all. As they stand up and look around, they realize that they are, and always have been, grown-ups merely pretending to be children.

So, what will it take for us to experience this mysterious state of awakening? Nothing complicated. In fact, if the process seems complicated, most likely the ego has taken over, in which case it is probably best to stop trying. In fact, letting go and allowing is the best practice. The following are a few tips for facilitating what is a simple, natural journey, the journey Home.

Partner Up

To wake up or return Home is an experience of re-joining, or reconnecting; therefore, it is contrary to the apparent experience of being a separate autonomous self. The independent self is very familiar, while the joined self is likely a new experience. The concept of a joined self seems contrary, even belittling, to the separated sense of self that has worked so hard to survive on its own, independently from its Source. Yet, to connect with guidance is the simplest way to feel the love that is inherent in true joining and obtain the support that awaits when we decide to give up the game of separation. It can be helpful to remember that when we join with an awakened one, we are expanding our awareness into Reality, into the full conscious awareness we are seeking.

Choose Peace

An important condition for facilitating the healing of the mind is peace—true peace, that is, not to be confused with false peace, the ego's version. True peace is not the contentment that comes from seeing hopes, dreams and wishes come true, or having a nice, manageable life or playing a good game; these would be evidence of ego satisfaction or false peace. True peace is not a lifestyle to aspire to, one day, later in life, when things are less hectic, nor is it the avoidance of drama that stems from fear and a desire for control. Take away the game, change up the situation and remove the ability to control and manage, and, if peace disappears, know that what was being experienced was not true peace. To settle for false peace is to fall for a trick of the ego.

True peace remains unshaken even when dreams are shattered. The importance of peace should not be underestimated because it is a mind at peace that bridges the gap to awakening. It is when we are at peace that we can most easily join with guidance, witness the divinity in our brothers and sisters and experience our Oneness with all of creation. Without it, truth, healing, wholeness and love cannot be fully experienced. Since peace is an inherent quality of true Self, it is possible to be in the middle of chaos and not lose peace. In all cases, if a situation has cost you your peace, know that the price was too high.

As humanity shifts toward greater awareness, it is not surprising that we are being flooded with a never-ending barrage of stimulating distractions. From the perspective of the ego, peace will be perceived as boring, even undesirable; if life is not exciting or thrilling, you are not fully alive. It may take a little vigilance to catch those moments when peace has been declined in favour of an exciting ego distraction. Because it places us in our right mind—that part of us that knows the truth of our divine existence—the ego will never choose peace and, in fact, will do whatever it can to distract us from peace. To say yes to peace is to shut down the ego's main avenue of communication. To the ego, peace is dangerous—peace is to the ego what Kryptonite is to Superman.

For those who are caught up in the rush of daily life, peace can appear as little more than a nice thought, certainly not something to be experienced on a daily basis. Minimize the distractions, simplify your life if necessary, so you can make time for what truly matters, for what requires your attention in the moment. It may be helpful to include a peaceful activity in your daily schedule, something simple and enjoyable, like a walk in the park, dabbling in a hobby, a simple exercise routine or yoga practice, meditation or a little time out for listening to soothing music. It should be an activity that does not carry a reward other than peace, something that cannot be measured or compared, in other words, an activity that the ego cannot grab onto for validation and satisfaction. You may experience during these quiet, peaceful times an increased flow of inspiration, creative and innovative solutions to problems that seemed impossible to resolve or a renewed sense of self-appreciation. These activities will reacquaint you with your true Self and make it easier to choose peace the next time you are drawn away from it.

Practise Quiet Mindfulness

Replace the habit of undisciplined, superfluous, senseless, unconscious thinking with quiet mindfulness. Become aware of how the ego churns out useless chatter, always for the purpose of keeping our attention focused on the dream. In order to break this habit, there must be a sincere desire to replace the limited awareness derived from independent thinking with an experience of full conscious awareness. Pay attention to the mind and watch for when it has wandered back to the game being played in the human condition, or the dream, so that it can gently be guided back. We choose where we place our attention, and there are only two options: in the dream or in Reality. This level of mindfulness requires being in a state of peace and is made easier when joined with guidance. It is a choice made in favour of your true Self—the one who deserves to experience full conscious awareness.

Let Go

The best way to facilitate awakening is to give up attempting to make it happen and simply allow what is natural and inevitable to take its course. This may be the most difficult aspect of the journey of awakening because it will not be pleasing to the ego. Since we have simply forgotten our true nature as whole expressions of the Infinite Life Source, God, Father/Mother, there is no need to take control, ferret out obstacles, dig up fears, errors, misunderstandings and false beliefs. To go on an internal witch hunt is a delaying tactic as well as an attempt at controlling the process, courtesy of the ego. As the next boundary is reached, whatever is blocking awakening will rise to the surface and be released without effort.

Be Curious

If there is one quality that will keep us on track for awakening, it is curiosity. To be like the child—open, curious and eager to explore what Life has to offer—is to engage in the ideal frame of mind. Being curious will facilitate and accelerate awakening because it takes attention away from the ego's need to manage the process. To be curious is to be ready to face the unknown, a position in which the ego has little, or even better, no control. To engage even a little curiosity about what lies beyond the limited human condition is to be on the right path, turned away from the dream toward Reality.

Ease Up

Love yourself enough to appreciate your current level of knowing, no matter how insignificant it seems. This is where your next learning opportunity awaits. Love yourself enough to brush off the mistakes you will make along the way. Since this is a journey in a new direction, mistakes will be made. When a mistake is made, forgive yourself and keep moving forward. What is important is to be engaged in the forward movement. There is no place for guilt on this journey; guilt is only another ego distraction.

Ease up on those with whom you share your daily activities, for they too are at their current level of best knowing. Love them enough to give them the space to expand their boundaries of awareness at the pace that best suits them. Just as you would not scold a toddler for stumbling upon taking his first steps, do not berate yourself or others for mistakes made within a dream or made-up condition. It is the shift in perception, the choice for seeing in another way, that will bring the desired correction.

Get Involved

Engage in activities you enjoy, something you care about, usually those activities that highlight your innate skills and abilities. Go out into the world and be the presence of love; be the light; share the Spirit of God being you. There is so much beauty in you, so much good, so much to be shared. In giving of yourself, you will discover who you are as God is being you. Remind yourself that if you exist at all, you have a purpose, for the Father/Mother only expresses that which has purpose.

Those who think they have seemingly insignificant lives, that they could not possibly have anything to contribute to the healing of humanity, underestimate the power of their presence. There is always something that can be done. Wake up, go for a walk in your neighbourhood, visit the shops, interact with people, practise seeing what God is being in your brothers and sisters. This is the quickest way to enhance and facilitate awakening. When you look for God in your brother's eyes, you are in the presence of God.

While making the gift of yourself is a wonderful way to discover what God is being in you, there are some, women mostly, who give far more of themselves than is called for. Excessive giving is usually practised in the hope of earning approval from others and is an indicator of lack of self-worth. It is a bargaining tool—essentially, it is a call for love. However, since the gift is usually received by those who identify with ego rather than Soul, it rarely, if ever, yields the desired result. If you dishonour yourself—which is always little more than an ego suggestion—others will dishonour you. If you want to be respected by others, respect yourself first. You are a son or daughter of God and deserve the utmost respect; self-sacrifice is never called for. The true gift comes from love, something that can be expressed only when self-love is first experienced.

Embracing the Possibilities

I was curious about how and why changing our mind or changing our way of seeing could actually have an impact on the world. My Friend had this to say. "The reason that changing your mind has an impact on the world you perceive is because it's all happening in the mind. Do not underestimate the power of your thoughts. This is what mind training is for. The sooner you turn your mind to the Father, and you stop thinking and apply yourself to being curious about what the Father is being, the sooner you will have an experience of what the Father is being.

"If you carry expectations and memories about how things are or how you think they should be, you will experience those things that you expect to experience. If you remove any expectations and memories, your experience will be wholly new; you will experience what God is being in the moment. How things will be expressed physically is inconsequential; physical expression is simply evidence or the consequence of either thinking or being from mind. Pay attention to your thinking, let it go, be from mind and the evidence will reveal change and support a new experience.

"The only thing that is truly worthy of your attention is to be curious about Reality, to want to know what more is available to be experienced. Once you are awake, you no longer have any barriers to your experience. Having abandoned all limited learning and memory, if you need to be in another place, for example, you will be in another place. You will simply teleport there. And when your business is finished, you simply return home."

Wow, this sounds incredible, and I let my imagination run with the possibilities. Since the world as we perceive it reflects our beliefs about ourselves, as we choose to embrace our divinity and invite our wholeness into our experience, we will find our bodies, our lives and the world around us conforming to our new choice. From within the dream of separation, it is difficult to imagine what waking up will mean in our lives, but we can imagine how wonderful it will be. If, as expressions of a loving Source, we collectively agree that our planet should be a place of safety, opportunity, abundance and well-being for all, we will have a world devoid of pollution, threat or danger of any kind. We will have a world where all needs are met in a graceful, harmonious and enjoyable manner and where each brother and sister experiences a sense of purpose and belonging. Since we are Mind, we may learn to communicate without the need of communication devices; since wholeness is our birthright, we will experience complete healing, where even the most advanced disease had set in. The possibilities are endless.

Being a practical person—I know, it sounds strange, a practical person who wants to experience enlightenment—I understood that waking up is a 100% deal, not 95% or 99%—it is a 100% experience. Anything less, if even a hint of fear or doubt remains, it is impossible to be from that place of infinite, limitless possibilities. I also understood that, while these visions of a better world were really exciting, the fact remains that the full experience of Reality is likely to be far greater than anything we could possibly imagine in our current state. That being the case, my Friend pointed out, it might be best not to speculate, lest we end up with a bunch of new expectations, definitions and beliefs.

> WE are the joint will of the Sonship, whose wholeness is for all. We begin the journey back by setting out TOGETHER, and gather in our brothers as we CONTINUE together. Every gain in our strength is offered for all, so they, too, can lay aside their weakness and add their strength to us. (ACIM, Chap. 8, p. 184)

What the World Needs Now

What the world needs now is love, as the song goes, but that will only happen as the ego frame of reference is abandoned and a new perspective is chosen. What the world really needs is brothers and sisters who have the courage to abandon old beliefs and embrace a radical new way of being as whole, infinite expressions of the One Mind. We believe that the world is bound by immutable laws, by forces of nature and cycles of growth and evolution over which we have limited or no control. However, since the world as we perceive it from within the frame of reference of the human condition is a world of our own making, we are only bound by the laws we have imagined and choose to cling to; they are not real, therefore not irrefutable. The structures and the laws of our world serve only to sustain the illusion of separation as defined by the ego sense of self.

As we shift our attention to our true Self as Mind and begin to trust our inherent divine nature, full conscious awareness will emerge and our experience of the world will change. As we reconnect with the Self, our experience of life shifts toward greater ease, fulfillment, peace, joy and healing. A sense of belonging emerges and participation in the world grows more meaningful and much more enjoyable. By releasing our definitions and beliefs, the world will gradually cease to be limited by the laws we have established, and it will blossom into its full splendour and greatness. A world of infinite possibilities awaits those souls brave enough to wonder if there might be more. The Real world is devoid of struggle, suffering, pain, lack, illness and death; it is a world of light, peace, love, wholeness, abundance, effortless unfolding and eternal life, and it is available right now to all who dare to let it in.

If any real change is to occur in the world, we will need to be courageous enough to explore unfamiliar territory—full conscious awareness. The current state of limitation, as is experienced in the human condition, is a state of ignorance or poor vision; it is not a natural or even necessary condition. It is the result of a choice made out of misguided curiosity, a choice we made—and continue to make—simply because we are free to do so; we always remain free to make a different choice. Like the early pioneers who were ready to test the prevailing belief that the world was flat, we now need to test our beliefs about the human condition and explore what we truly are as Mind.

Humanity stands at a threshold; we need a few adventurous souls who are willing to be the presence of love in the world. In the light of your presence, others will know that there is a different choice to be made, a choice they too can make so they can be the presence of love for the brothers and sisters they interact with on a daily basis. The best way to be in the world is to play the game without taking it too seriously, to engage in a job and activities that best reflect your unique skills and abilities. From what I have seen in consultation, most men and women have a sense of their true function in life. By abandoning the senseless quest for worldly success and allowing your Being to emerge, you will make the greatest contribution of all: what the Infinite Life Source is being in you.

If you are still reading, perhaps you have gathered up sufficient courage, maybe ignited some curiosity about what it is that needs to be done next. In a way, we are pioneers, moving into what seems like unchartered territory, but what we are doing is moving out of fantasy into what is our normal territory—Reality. Some of my clients have shared that none of their friends understand their quest for awakening, and they feel alone on their journey, which is understandable, since this is a new direction for humanity. Interestingly, while working on this section, I caught the title of the song playing on the radio: "Between Friends." Just as our brothers and sisters need examples of how to be in a new way, we too need friends as we embrace this unique new way of being. Because the nature of our Source is Love, we are never left without the support we need. When sincerely engaged on this journey of healing and awakening, somehow, we attract fellow seekers. Together, we can, and will, contribute to the healing of humanity. Will you be among us?

Positions Available: Seeking bold, adventurous souls who are ready and willing to replace outdated beliefs with a radically new view of life to contribute to the healing of humanity.

An Invitation

Dear Brothers and Sisters,

Please accept this invitation to be the Presence of Love. It is a one-time invitation, but, due to its divine nature, it will never expire. You may accept it now, you may ignore it awhile, or you may reject it outright, but you cannot destroy it. It is a seed planted in the fertile ground of your Soul, and since the substance of your Being is Love, it cannot be destroyed.

This is an invitation to release all grievances and ancient hurts. There is no cost other than the cost of abandoning resistance to Love. Because being the Presence of Love is natural, it is healing for yourself and for everyone you encounter every day of your life. There are no limitations to love, for it is infinite. Love waits simply for your acceptance.

Flowers in the Desert

Michael J. Miller

In a barren place
Where nothing grows or lives
A strange sight I did see:
Out of the drought-stricken ground
Arose a rose
How could it be?
In this place without hope or laughter
Something beautiful could still be?
I marvelled at the sight
Could barely believe it through my tears of joy
And then a strange thing happened:
Another flower appeared,
And then another and another,
Until fields of vibrant colour stretched as far as the eye could see!
All blooming as I laid my eyes on them,
And a song started to rise
Like I had not heard in a long time;
And suddenly I realized
This desert had all along been
A beautiful garden.
Only when I wanted to see it,
Did I.

Bibliography

All references to *A Course in Miracles* are from the Sparkly Edition. Available for download or purchase online at http://acimsearch.org/get-a-sparkly.

Campbell, Joseph. *The Power of Myth*. NY: Anchor Books Doubleday, 1988.

Edward, Pauline. *Choosing the Miracle*. Montreal: Desert Lily Publications, 2012.

———. *The Movement of Being*. Montreal: Desert Lily Publications, 2014.

Lawrence, Brother. *The Practice of the Presence of God and the Spiritual Maxims*. Mineola, NY: Dover Publications, Inc., 2005.

Merton, Thomas. *The Seven Storey Mountain*. Orlando, FL: Harcourt Brace Jovanovich, Inc., 1976.

Tuttle, Paul Norman. *Graduation: The End of Illusions*. Kingston: The Northwest Foundation for *A Course in Miracles*, 1991.

ONLINE RESOURCES

Please visit the author's website for links,
book reviews and additional resources.
www.paulineedward.com

Ego Flare-up Emergency Extinguishers

From *Choosing the Miracle*

Although a simple "no" will suffice when it comes to addressing an ego flare-up, being unrelenting and increasingly clever in its efforts to attract and maintain our attention, it can be helpful to have a few spare emergency responses when we feel we have lost control. Here is a list of some of my favourite ego flare-up emergency extinguishers. Feel free to add your own to this list.

- Tell yourself that God loves you, no matter what, besides which, you haven't failed because you never left home in the first place. Chances are that the ego will have a few snarky comebacks, so, move on to the next item on this list.
- Ask: Father, what is the truth here? And if that doesn't work, move on down the list.
- Forgive yourself. If you could have done it right the first time, you wouldn't be in this situation in the first place.
- Flip the switch on the ego, and move on.
- Don't analyze; you'll only be analyzing a decision made in a moment of insanity. Now, how sane is that?
- You are not the ego; the ego is no more than a bad habit.
- Remind yourself that you are the boss! The ego is a work of fiction, made up by a scared child, the part of you that is asleep.
- Be quiet and ask for help.
- Be quiet and listen for help.
- Be quiet and expect to receive help.
- Although this may be difficult at first, try peace, the ego's kryptonite.
- Don't look back; just keep moving forward.
- Find a distraction, something fun to do, something that is more important than analyzing your screw-up.
- The ego analyzes; the Holy Spirit accepts.

- Remind yourself that your brother/sister is just like you, afraid of love.
- I am never upset for the reason I think.
- The ego always lies; don't even bother trying to reason with it.
- Don't ruminate, cogitate or try to understand why you messed up. You left your wholeness for a moment because you were afraid of love. Period.
- Your brother/sister is calling for love. If that doesn't motivate you to choose peace, see next point.
- We go home together, or not at all. Awakening is a two-person job.
- Choosing the miracle is a habit. It undoes the bad habit of choosing to believe the ego's lies.
- In case you missed it, just keep moving forward!
- Go for a walk, listen to music, have a cookie or two or three.
- Call a friend or family member and talk about something that concerns them.
- Do not bring this up for analysis with your therapist, don't text it to your BFF. The point is to deflate it, and the only way to do that is to not give it any attention.
- The ego thrives and survives on the attention you give it.
- Remind yourself that your real job is to be the light for your brothers and sisters. Do it for them.
- Treat yourself, your brothers and sisters, every object, animate or inanimate, with dignity and respect, for all there is before you is God and His creation.

If none of this works, enjoy the ego flare-up, wallow in it, bask in it, but don't feel guilty about it. Then, try to recall what it feels like to be at peace. Peace probably feels much better than an ego flare-up. Next time, you'll choose differently. God loves you. Now, move forward.

Tips for Working with Guidance

From *The Movement of Being*

Working with a guide is easy, and also fun. When exploring a new way of being, it is most helpful to have a loving, understanding friend by our side. Feel free to be yourself; don't be shy. Ask whatever questions you need for clarification.

- Don't think about it or wonder if the whole thing might not be a little bit over the top or too esoteric for you; just do it!
- Persist. You are not likely to be successful on the first try, especially if you are new to meditation and connecting with guidance.
- It's never about the problem or the question; it's about joining.
- Avoid the temptation to analyze or question the validity of the information you receive. Instead, see how it feels.
- Become familiar with the ego's language and proclivities. It will be easier to differentiate its voice from that of your guide.
- The voice for truth always comes from peace.
- The ego's advice will not likely lead to peace. It may lead to temporary joy, self-satisfaction or exhilaration, but that is not peace.
- Your guide is your equal, your friend; don't be afraid to express yourself as you would with a dear friend.
- Expect simple, practical solutions and insights.
- Ask your question and then leave it alone. The answer may come when you least expect it, very likely when you are quiet, unconcerned and peaceful.
- Practise with simple questions.
- The practice of joining with guidance gradually breaks the habit of self-protection and isolation.
- Don't be afraid to question the guidance you receive and ask for further clarification when it appears unclear.

- Your guide's function is to be of assistance; it is therefore most wise to seek out and welcome that assistance.
- The more diligent you are in developing a quiet mind, the easier it will be to listen for guidance.
- It's never about the answer or the outcome; it's about joining.
- Joining greatly speeds up awakening.
- Accept the gift of guidance, for in your acceptance the joining has been made complete.

The Movement of Being
Pauline Edward
Desert Lily Publications, Montreal, Canada

Whether we are aware of it or not, each moment of our lives holds all that is needed for the complete unfolding of our Being. Still, there are those periods when the evidence of this unfolding seems to leap to our awareness, taking us completely by surprise, even causing us to stumble and fall as long-held ancient beliefs crumble beneath our feet. These moments force us to reach beyond the safety of failing familiar frontiers, leaving us open to awakening to what has been there all along. These are the moments shared by the author as she prepares to sell her beloved home and move to a condo. While connecting with guidance and exploring the possibility of her own awakening, she shares her encounters with the Love that has always been and will always remain the Source of our very Being. This book is the fourth in a series that began with *Making Peace with God*.

"'I was cracked. No more withholding…no more trying to fix myself…There was only Being. I did a little rumba at the far end of the dining room. Cracked. What joy! What relief!' This is how Pauline Edward describes the end of her struggle and tribulations through a turbulent journey of Awakening. What a privilege it is to be invited, as the reader, into the Journey towards Awakening, written by an honest and committed graduate of *A Course in Miracles*! Deeply personal, touching and often funny, Pauline generously shares her experiences of being human, seeking liberation from self-imposed concepts and beliefs with the goal to be free and Be Love. *The Movement of Being* is a practical guide for those who are tired of wrestling with the same old patterns—over and over and over again, and ready to decide they want to Be the Love they are."
—Marlise Witschi, M.Psych.

"In this wonderful book, the author shares her journey with her brothers and sisters who are consciously engaged on the path of awakening. *The Movement of Being* clearly portrays the differences

between the right- and wrong-minded vantage points, and is most helpful for un-rutting false ego beliefs about ourselves. It provides clear insights on how to recognize Being, how to trust in Its Movement and how to experience the Movement of our own Being. Highly recommended for anyone on the path of awakening."
—Homer Lin, ACIM Taipei, Taiwan

"More people need to know that spiritual guidance is possible and to hear ways to receive guidance from those who do. Pauline has provided a personal and moving experience about her journey of awakening. *The Movement of Being* is filled with examples of how everyone can use each moment to step closer to their own shift in consciousness."
—Tim Alan Smith, author of *A Tiny Mad Idea*

"I loved this book. I finally found a book that resonated with my feelings about God/Jesus/the Universe and our place in it! I have always suspected that when we awaken, we don't disappear from this earth, but rather we actually LIVE it fully. It's as though we can see and experience beyond our limitations!! I have been a student of *A Course in Miracles* for years, and I often find myself at odds with some of the teachings about this concept. It was so wonderful to read your book. While reading, I kept shouting, 'Yes!!'
"This book is an awesome gift. I will cherish it. I will also recommend it to my clients, family, and friends. Beautiful, beautiful, beautiful."
—Constance Wells, Ph.D., Clinical Psychology, Integrated Therapy Center

Choosing the Miracle
Pauline Edward
Desert Lily Publications, Montreal, Canada

This book was nearly three quarters of the way finished when, seven years into her work with *A Course in Miracles*, the author hit a wall. Although it appeared as a very high wall that would take a very long time and a whole lot of effort to be climbed, as it turned out, it simply needed to be risen above and left behind. This passing hurdle resulted in the crumbling of a lifetime of learning and a major shift in perception, the ideal condition for a true experience of the miracle. Written with the same candour, sincerity, wit and courage, this book picks up where *Leaving the Desert* left off and will be an inspiration for all spiritual seekers.

"The greatest compliment an author of a spiritual book can receive is that their extension of love is felt throughout the book. I found that *Choosing the Miracle* not only inspired me, but gave me a direct experience of God."
—Reverend Dan Costello

"In *Choosing the Miracle*, Pauline Edward graciously plants yet another shimmering guidepost for her fellow Course students. By sharing the entertaining insights gleaned from her own ongoing growth with *A Course in Miracles*, Pauline Edward looks through the ceaseless lies of the ego to reveal the truth of spirit. Stay on Course by *Choosing the Miracle*."
—Alexander Marchand, author of *The Universe Is a Dream*

"*Choosing the Miracle* is a wonderful read for any serious student of *A Course in Miracles*. It reveals the true simplicity of the Course's message, and offers insight for applying the Course into our every day lives and every encounter. Moments of realization are ours to experience when we simply make the choice. And when we join Pauline Edward on her journey in *Choosing the Miracle* we witness the true simplicity in making the choice… the true simplicity of living the "Miracle.""

"In *Choosing the Miracle* Pauline Edward not only shows us the simplicity of living *A Course in Miracles*, she shares with us, through her personal journey, how our Truth is right here, right now. No more waiting, no more searching. Enlightenment is not only for a select few. It is not out of our reach. It is for everyone, right here, right now!

"If you've read *A Course in Miracles* over, maybe completed the Workbook lessons more than once and you are done with baby steps and are now hungry to witness the Truth every day of your life, then I recommend reading Pauline Edward's book *Choosing the Miracle*. The message is powerful. Heaven is right here, right now. Why wait a minute longer? When you can be CHOOSING the MIRACLE today!

"*Choosing the Miracle* is a wonderful account of the simplicity of actually "living" *A Course in Miracles*, and opens the door for dedicated students who are WILLING to live and walk the Truth right here, right now, TODAY!"

—Robyn Busfield, Author of *Forgiveness Is the Home of Miracles*

Leaving the Desert
Embracing the Simplicity of *A Course in Miracles*
Pauline Edward
Desert Lily Publications, Montreal, Canada

After completing a first reading of *A Course in Miracles*, the most challenging read of her life, the author exclaimed, "Never again!" Yet, she knew that if she were to make real progress with her lifelong spiritual quest, she would need a thorough understanding of the Course's unique thought system. So, back to school she went—the school of life, that is. Though a seasoned seeker, never did she anticipate the dark nights she would encounter along the journey, nor the gift of grace that would pull her through. Readers will delight in the same profound spiritual insight, candour, humour and lively writing style as found in *Making Peace with God*.

"*Leaving the Desert: Embracing the Simplicity of A COURSE IN MIRACLES*, is one of the most practical spiritual books ever written. I was struck by Pauline's ability to clearly and simply state the principles of the Course, from the beginning of her journey, through a genuine spiritual search, to her discovery of a new direction, to the understanding of miracles, and ultimately to the miracle of forgiveness in undoing the deviousness of the ego. I highly recommend this book to anyone who is on a spiritual path, and especially to those who want to get on the fast track."
—Gary Renard, Best-selling author of *The Disappearance of the Universe*

"I thoroughly enjoyed *Leaving the Desert* by Pauline Edward. It is an excellent description of the basic metaphysics and psychology of *A Course in Miracles* and its practical application in daily life, written in a clear conversational style."
—Jon Mundy, Ph.D., author of *Living A COURSE IN MIRACLES*

"In *Leaving the Desert: Embracing the Simplicity of A COURSE IN MIRACLES*, Pauline Edward shares her intimate quest both to fully comprehend the Course's fundamental principles despite the ego's formidable resistance and to apply its unique forgiveness in her

daily life. *Leaving the Desert* will inspire Course newbies and veterans alike with its profound, comprehensive understanding and specific examples fearlessly and generously drawn from the classroom of the author's life."
—Susan Dugan, author of *Extraordinary Ordinary Forgiveness*

"Written with humor and courageous self-disclosure, Pauline Edward's *Leaving the Desert* is a delight. Through sharing her own exploration—her commitment and her doubts—she addresses all the major topics covered in *A Course in Miracles* with precision and clarity. For new students as well as veterans of the Course, her overview of its purpose and methodology is excellent. Her adroit sprinkling of personal anecdotes enlivens and clarifies her path (and ours) and her honesty allows the book to be a comforting companion to those seeking to engage more artfully with this life-changing practice. You will read this book with a smile of recognition and gratitude."
—Carol Howe, author of *Never Forget to Laugh: Personal Recollections of Bill Thetford, Co-scribe of A COURSE IN MIRACLES*

"Pauline Edward delivers the concepts of *A Course in Miracles* elegantly and uncompromisingly, and with an undeniably gifted style. This book is wonderful. It offers a deep and much-needed exploration of the core message of *A Course in Miracles*. It comes from profound guidance, and places the reader at the altar of Truth. *Leaving the Desert* is a must-read for any student of the Course, or any person seeking enlightenment, who would leave no stone unturned in an endeavour to return Home to our natural state of Love."
—Robyn Busfield, author of *Forgiveness Is the Home of Miracles*

Making Peace with God
The Journey of a *Course in Miracles* Student
Pauline Edward
Desert Lily Publications, Montreal, Canada

It is said, "Seek and you will find." But what happens when your quest for the truth about life, God and the meaning of existence repeatedly fails to offer satisfactory answers? Determined to uncover the truth, you persist, and, lo and behold, you find. But what if the truth you discover challenges each and every one of your beliefs? This is the story of one woman's lifelong search for a fulfilling spirituality, one that answers the unanswerable, that is truly universal and all-inclusive and, above all, that is logical and practicable. *Making Peace with God* recounts a journey that begins with Roman Catholicism, explores various ancient and contemporary spiritualities and culminates with the extraordinary thought system of *A Course in Miracles*.

Gary Renard, best-selling author of *The Disappearance of the Universe*, highly recommends this wonderful book.

"A must read for *A Course in Miracles* students or anyone curious about its profound, mind-healing message."
—Susan Dugan, author of *Extraordinary Ordinary Forgiveness*

"*Making Peace with God* is the ultimate destination of all spiritual journeys… a story sure to save much time for the spiritual seeker."
—Alexander Marchand, author and artist of *The Universe Is a Dream: The Secrets of Existence Revealed*

"An inspiring and enjoyable book which will encourage others on their spiritual journey."
—Michael Dawson, author of *Healing the Cause*

"I recommend *Making Peace with God* to anyone who would like good company on the path!"
—Jennifer Hadley

The Power of Time
Understanding the Cycles of Your Life's Path
Pauline Edward
Llewellyn Worldwide, Ltd. Woodbury, MN

Don't wait around for life to just "happen." Develop a solid, successful life plan with guidance from astrologer-numerologist Pauline Edward. Whether your goals are personal or professional, *The Power of Time* will help you take advantage of the powerful natural cycles at work in your life. Simple calculations based on numerology reveal where you are in each nine-year cycle and what to expect from each year, month and day. With your life path clearly mapped out, it will be easy for you to pinpoint the best times to start a new job, focus on family, launch a business, take time to reflect, make a major purchase, complete a project, expand your horizons and more.

"I've used numerology for nearly 30 years. This tool is accurate, exciting, and helpful. *The Power of Time* will show you how."
—Christiane Northrup, MD, author of *Women's Bodies, Women's Wisdom* and *The Wisdom of Menopause*

"A top-notch reference, one that will excite and instruct anyone about the power of numbers in your life."
—*Dell Horoscope*

"This immensely readable book is a fascinating introduction to the subject of numerology. Best of all, *The Power of Time* takes the reader by the hand and shows her how to apply the concepts to her own life. I found the workbook sections especially helpful and could not put the book down until I had charted my own Life Path Number, Personal Year Number and 9-Year Epicycle. *The Power of Time* is a unique and insightful contribution to the many books available on setting goals and making short- and long-term career plans."
—CJ Carmichael, best-selling romance author

Astrological Crosses
Exploring the Cardinal, Fixed and Mutable Modes
Pauline Edward
Desert Lily Publications, Montreal, Canada

For the first time ever, here is an astrology book that focuses on astrological crosses (the cardinal, fixed and mutable aspects of the signs of the zodiac) and their impact on people's lives, behaviour, actions and motivation. Crosses are so important to truly understanding a chart that you will wonder how you ever completed an astrological analysis without this essential component. *Astrological Crosses in Relationships* explores the strengths and challenges of each cross, using many real-life stories taken from the author's consulting practice. With this innovative guide, you can learn to identify crosses in everyday life experiences, mend star-crossed relationships and balance a lack or overemphasis of crosses in your birth chart.

"Pauline Edward's book helps us understand why people think and communicate the way they do, which in turn helps us to improve our relationships. That's no small feat! In-depth, well-written, and informative... A valuable asset to anyone interested in understanding human behaviour."
—Lucy MacDonald, MEd, author of *Learn to Be an Optimist*

"The best book yet about the nature of cardinal, fixed, and mutable. Her readable, insightful work can help both beginning and experienced astrologers gain much understanding about life's processes. Highly recommended."
—Michael Munkasey, PMAFA, NCGR-IV

"Absolutely excellent work on the cardinal, fixed and mutable qualities of the signs. Suitable for any level of astrologer, this goes into the subject at a deeper level than I've seen before. Thought-provoking and intelligently written."
—*The Wessex Astrologer*

About the Author

Pauline Edward is an astrologer-numerologist, speaker and Certified Professional Coach and Group Leader. She is the recipient of a Chamber of Commerce Accolades Award for excellence in business practice. With a background in the sciences and a fascination for all things mystical, Pauline's journey has been enriched by a wide range of experiences from research in international economics, technical writing in R & D and computer training, to studies in astrology, numerology, meditation, yoga, shamanism, the Bach Flower Remedies, herbology, healing and reiki. Her lifelong quest for truth and an understanding of the meaning of life eventually led her to *A Course in Miracles*, a teaching that has now become an integral part of her life.

Pauline is available for consultations, coaching, speaking engagements and workshops. For information about services, upcoming events and publications, visit her website: www.paulineedward.com.

Printed in Great Britain
by Amazon